MASSACRE ON THE ROAD TO DUNKIRK

Wormhout 1940

Massacre on the Road to Dunkirk

WORMHOUT 1940

Leslie Aitken, MBE

PATRICK STEPHENS

First published in 1977

Second edition 1988

British Library Cataloguing in
Publication Data

Aitken, Leslie
Massacre on the road to Dunkirk:
Wormhout, 1940.
1, France, Wormhout. Great Britain.
Army. Atrocities by Leibstandarte
Adolf Hitler, 1939-1945.
I. Title
940.54'05'094427

ISBN 1 85260 185 X

Patrick Stephens Limited is part of the
Thorsons Publishing Group, Wellingborough,
Northamptonshire NN8 2RQ, England.

Printed in Great Britain by
Baker, Land and Unwin Printing,
Wellingborough, Northamptonshire

1   3   5   7   9   10   8   6   4   2

*Dedicated to
all members of the Forces
of the Crown
past and present
and to whom Great Britain
owes more
than is ever acknowledged*

List of Illustrations

Maps and Diagrams

Contents

Appendix:

Foreword

by Jeff Rooker, MP

Many people and especially the author of this book have tried for years to assemble enough of the jigsaw of Wormhout to force action. It is now beyond doubt that the pieces are sufficient, as the pages which follow will show. At long last the spotlight of history is upon Wormhout.

The events portrayed in this book took place before I was born. Reading them should leave those in high places, both civilian and military, uncomfortable. The general reader will have feelings of both pride and anger.

Pride in the sheer heroism of those who readily went to war — unprepared by those in command of the nation. Anger at the apparent indifference for almost 50 years to the massacre at Wormhout.

The Third Reich was seeking to rule our planet for a thousand years by force and terror. It had to be stopped. The Nazis mis-read the British nature as a sign of weakness. The remnants of Nazism and any would-be Nazis will surely see it as a sign of unmistakable strength that we will not close a file while justice is undone.

It is to be hoped that the politicians who make the rules of war will not allow the rules of international politics to be used to avoid the justice which this book demands. For the few survivors of Wormhout the memories are long and the passage of time is no excuse for inaction.

A deaf ear to the dead and the survivors is also a deaf ear to everyone else who made the supreme sacrifice to end Nazi rule in Europe.

JEFF ROOKER
House of Commons, London SW1

Acknowledgements

Acknowledgement is due to the authors and publishers of the following books for permission to quote certain extracts: Cassell & Co. Ltd., for *The Second World War* by Winston Churchill; Clarke, Irwin & Co. Ltd (Toronto), for *The Trial of Kurt Meyer,* by B. J. S. MacDonald; Evans Brothers (Books) Ltd, for *The London Cage,* by Lt.-Col. A. Scotland, OBE; Martin Secker & Warburg Ltd. for *The Order of the Death's Head*, by Heinz Hohne, translated by Richard Barry; Leo Cooper Ltd., for *Massacre at Malmedy,* by Charles Whiting.

Also to: The Public Record Office, for help in tracing War Diaries; the Imperial War Museum, for permission to reproduce photographs; the Judge Advocate General, for permission to use letters and quote from affidavits of British survivors; Lt.-Col. M. Ryan, OBE, St John's House, Warwick, for permission to quote from the Regimental Diary and other material; Colonel L. T. Tomes, OBE, for permission to quote from *Personal Diary of events between May 10th and June 17th, 1940,* the Mayor and Conseiller, Esquelbecq, for general information and advice; the Weiner Library, London, for information concerning Sepp Dietrich, etc.; Mr D. Cordrey, for material and photographs; Mr Brian Davis, for permission to reproduce photographs of the *Leibstandarte* – SS Regt.

War Diary (WO 167/839): Quotations from this Crown-copyright record in the Public Record Office appear by permission of the Controller of H.M. Stationery Office.

Preface

The climax of this true story is the massacre by SS-troops of nearly a hundred men in a barn at Esquelbecq, together with the murder and maltreatment of others, during the Battle of Wormhout. It is set within the story of their participation in the Battle of France 1940. Its significance is the holding operation at Wormhout, which contributed to the escape of many troops from the beaches of Dunkirk – and the reaction of those who were frustrated by the resistance of a much smaller force.

I have tried to set down those events which led to the travail of the man in khaki who quite often perceived nothing more than a 'typical bloody Army mess-up'. But the war with its chaotic happenings stemmed from the demands of voters for a reduction in armaments and the Treaty of Versailles. The man in uniform was faced, in the Second World War, with dying for policies which had failed – and of which almost everyone had approved.

To set the massacre in its context, it was necessary for me to explain how the British came to be outnumbered at Wormhout, and how they got there. Likewise, the German unit involved has been followed across Europe on its victory trail to Wormhout, and because of its importance as an SS-unit, something of its history has been related.

The bibliography and notes will shew how indebted I am to the authorities and sources I have consulted, and each item occurs in chronological order as employed in the text. The only footnotes are in respect of direct quotations.

I first heard the story of the massacre from Bill and Douglas Cordrey in May 1972, on my return from Le Paradis with Major-General D.A. Wade, after dedicating a memorial to the men of the Royal Norfolk Regiment who were massacred there. The Cordreys were in Dunkirk in order to re-visit nearby Wormhout, and when Douglas shewed me a list of four or five survivors of the Massacre at Wormhout I said that we ought to try and trace them in case any were in need of help.

When all the survivors whose names appear in this story were traced, I discovered that hardly anyone had believed their accounts. This was due, in part, to the absence of the massacre from much of the literature dealing with the Battle of France, and so I sought to repair the omission.

Another reason why the story has received little publicity, is that no one was brought to trial. Although the requisite of most novels is that crime should not go unpunished, it appears that in real life the guilty can sometimes go free . . . Arising from this is the need to preserve the anonymity of those few Germans whose accounts could be used against them by fanatical ex-Nazis, or others seeking vengeance. They are referred to by pseudonyms, and the list of these appears after this preface.

It would have been difficult to have proceeded without the provision of material by Douglas Cordrey who, being resident in London, has undertaken journeys to various places in order to feed me with information, without complaint. Many of the excellent photographs are his work. I am also grateful to Colonel L. T. Tomes, for the provision of his private diary and permission to quote freely from it. Also, the Commanding Officer of the Royal Warwickshire Regiment has kindly allowed me to quote from the Regimental History, and use other material. Mr William Cordrey's personal reminiscences have been useful as background information. Mrs G. Rothwell's help with German translation was invaluable and I am grateful to Miss J. Dines, for drawing excellent maps and to my wife, for help with research problems.

The survivors have, in nearly every case, been most considerate in allowing me to question them on many occasions, and at odd times. Three men suffered my calling on them over twenty times each – and we are still friends!

None of the survivors has indicated any feelings of resentment towards the German people, so this account is not the reflection of any bitterness which some might assume to exist in the hearts of men who suffered so terribly.

After so many years, it is natural that certain details supplied by those who were in the massacre should differ – in such cases I have settled for the view which is common to the majority.

Like the Memorial to those who died in the massacre, the telling of this story to a wide public is overdue.

Leslie Aitken

The names of the following are pseudonyms:
Seven Company guards: Ritter, Schauff, Dorn, Scheide
Eight Company guards: Koriaka
On attachment: SS-Hauptsturmführer Alfred Ebner

CHAPTER ONE

Hitler's Favourite Soldiers

The month of May in the year 1939 was to prove fateful for the whole world. It was on 23rd May that Hitler summoned his military chiefs to Berlin to inform them that, as Poland was purported to have broken the non-aggression pact with Germany, that pact was now void. Consequently, Poland would be invaded at the first available opportunity – this notwithstanding Neville Chamberlain's declaration that in the event of a German attack Britain and France would go to the aid of Poland.

For the purpose of his military career, it was a momentous month for SS-Hauptsturmführer Otto Baum as, less than a week after Hitler's meeting with the Generals, the Hauptsturmführer was excited to receive notice of a posting which filled him with pride, and was to take him to Berlin. At that time, he was stationed in Klagenfurt, Austria, as Commander of Ten Company, *Der Führer*-SS Infantry Regiment which was the fourth and most recent SS-Regiment, having been formed in 1938. But now, Otto Baum was to join the *Leibstandarte*-SS Adolf Hitler Regiment, as Commander of its Seven Company.

He boarded the train for the long journey to Berlin with a measure of self-satisfaction, feeling honoured that he was about to join the senior SS-Regiment. There were several men whom he longed to meet, especially the *Leibstandarte's* Regimental Commander, SS-Obergruppenführer Josef 'Sepp' Dietrich.

Dietrich was an influential and colourful Nazi whose membership went back to the early days of the Party. Born in Hawengen on 28th May 1892, he belonged to a Bavarian peasant family and worked in the fields as a young boy. Feeling adven-

17

turous he ran away in his early teens to Munich, and became a butcher's apprentice.

In 1911, he joined the Imperial Army and during the 1914-18 war rose to the rank of Sergeant-Major and was awarded the Iron Cross, 1st Class. When the first tank was captured from the British, in 1916, he taught himself how to handle the huge, tracked vehicle and with some pride reckoned himself to have been one of the first Germans to realize the importance of the tank.

On demobilisation he found it hard to settle down as a civilian and was employed in various jobs, working as a waiter, policeman, foreman in a tobacco factory, customs officer and petrol-pump attendant. Also he became interested in the Trades Union movement, but forsook this to join the National Socialist German Workers' Party.

He became one of Hitler's closest supporters, and to the Führer he owed his meteoric rise in rank and importance. His temperament made him ideally suited to be chosen as one of the toughs who in the early days had the task of protecting their leader. As Hitler's car sped him to meetings which were often disturbed, it also contained the *chauffeureska* who were suitably equipped for the task with rubber truncheons and whips.

Amongst other work entrusted to Dietrich was the organisation of the SS in Southern Bavaria, but he owed his military function to his appointment as Hitler's chief bodyguard when the Nazis seized power. Hitler's selection of Dietrich was based on a shrewd assessment of his personal qualities, for in addition to being tough the ex-sergeant-major was possessed of no little courage.

On Hitler's instructions, Dietrich formed a unit of 120 carefully selected men, known as the SS-Headquarters Guard, Berlin. From this Praetorian Guard the *Leibstandarte* emerged when, at the Nuremberg Rally in September 1933, Hitler publicly named the Guard Battalion after himself. Two months later the *Leibstandarte* swore eternal allegiance to the Führer, whose private Army it had become.[1]

[1] A type of bodyguard had existed from March 1923, when a group of 'old fighters' undertook to protect Hitler from all enemies and called themselves the *Stabswache*. It was from these men that the SS stemmed, and their uniforms in-

During the Röhm Purge of 30th June 1934, Dietrich was entrusted with the direction of the executions in Stadelheim Prison. His standing in the Third Reich was such that he was said 'to know everyone, and everyone knew him'. He was of such a generous nature that it was acknowledged that those to whom he took a liking could have almost anything from him. In conversation, he employed highly colourful language and referred to people by their Christian names. If he used their surnames, they had incurred his displeasure.

Opinions of him ranged between that of William Shirer, who described him as 'one of the most brutal men in the Third Reich', to Field Marshal von Rundstedt's terse 'stupid, but decent'. Irrespective of the opinions of outsiders, he was a popular commander with the men under his leadership and not lacking in courage on the field of battle. He retained command of the *Leibstandarte* when successively it became a regiment, a brigade and a division. His popularity with ex-Nazis is such that at a meeting in Karlsburg on 29th July 1957, Kurt Meyer made a reference to him which received a tremendous ovation.

Before the war the solely ceremonial function of the *Leibstandarte* prompted critics to name its members 'the Ashphalt Soldiers'. Eventually Dietrich consented to his men being trained as fighting soldiers.

As in the case of members of other Waffen-SS units, recruits were required to be in perfect physical condition and over six feet in height. Each man was so carefully selected that the slightest physical blemish would disqualify him. Potential officers were required to serve in the ranks for two years, which produced a certain amount of criticism from officers of the Wehrmacht. Nevertheless, a close relationship was established between SS-officers and men.

Although the *Leibstandarte* and other SS-units sought to become the embodiment of the Nazi ideal, their independence and arrogance caused the Wehrmacht to regard them with no little dis-

---

cluded black ski-caps with a silver Death's Head badge and black-edged Swastika armbands.

favour. Quarrels between men of the Waffen-SS and the Army were frequent and the strained relationship between them could not be disguised.

As war approached, the men of the Waffen-SS became fanatically eager to demonstrate their military prowess and, moreover, to shew their readiness to die as well as to kill.

SS-Hauptsturmführer Otto Baum took over command of the *Leibstandarte's* Seven Company at the end of May 1939, and during the following three months participated in the normal exercises of a motorised infantry regiment.

On 1st September, the German forces which had been massed along the Polish border attacked at daybreak, the air attacks having begun an hour earlier. The *Leibstandarte* crossed the frontier near Gola and took part in the fighting near Borislavice, Vavjanice, the Varta crossing and in the area Kucno. Later, Dietrich's men participated in the attack on Warsaw (which held out until 28th September) but were diverted before the fall of Warsaw to the fortress of Modlin until it capitulated.

During the *Leibstandarte's* participation in the Battle of Warsaw, Otto Baum was awarded the Iron Cross, Second Class.

In the Polish campaign the *Leibstandarte* shared with other SS-units exceptionally heavy losses, which were considerably heavier than those of comparable Army formations. This led certain Army critics to ascribe these to a lack of military expertise, but it could not be said that the men of the Waffen-SS lacked courage. The casualties sustained by officers of the Waffen-SS were so heavy that replacements became necessary straight from the cadet schools.

After Modlin, the *Leibstandarte* moved on to Prague, where it remained until December and was then transferred to Western Germany, to be re-fitted and re-inforced.

CHAPTER TWO

Across France and Back

On 10th September 1939, the 2nd Battalion, Royal Warwickshire Regiment was in Aldershot, awaiting orders to proceed to France with the British Expeditionary Force. The war between Germany and the Allies was seven days old and the Battalion was up to strength, with 27 officers and 796 men. These were regular soldiers and re-called reservists, most of whom had served with the Regiment in India and Palestine.

Consisting of Battalion HQ and four Rifle Companies, its armament establishment was: 10 Bren carriers, 12 2-inch mortars, 2 3-inch mortars, 22 Boyes anti-tank rifles, 50 light machine-guns and 734 rifles, although on 10th September it was still deficient in equipment.

Brigaded with the 5th in the 2nd Infantry Division, Lieutenant-Colonel P. D. W. Dunn, DSO, MC, was its recently appointed Commanding Officer.

Farewells having been said to their families, the men sailed from Southampton on 23rd September, at 5.30 pm, and the crossing was rough, with many troops and even members of the crew suffering sea-sickness. Those who had expected attentions from the enemy in the Channel were surprised that they were troubled only by the rough sea, and everybody was glad to arrive safely in Cherbourg early on the 24th.

They left Cherbourg by train for their immediate destinations, with 'A', 'B' and 'C' Companies being billeted at Auvers le Hamon, 'D' Company at Ronceray Farm and HQ Company at Château de Varenne.

By early October the British 1st and 2nd Corps were safely

assembled in France, according to schedule; and on 2nd October the Battalion arrived at Achiet le Petit (Pas de Calais) and for three days most of the time was spent digging the first trenches.

On 5th October they moved up to Rumegies. By this time the BEF's line ran from Maulde (south of Tournai) to Halluin, with a lay-back flank position on the river Lys which extended from Halluin to Armentières. The French First Army was on the BEF's right, with the Seventh Army on its left.

The billets at Rumegies were good and as the Allied Commanders expected an imminent German invasion of Belgium, the men dug trenches, laid wire and built bunkers. This work was to occupy them until mid-November. During leisure moments the men enjoyed the hospitality of many local French people; and the *estaminets* were crowded with troops, whose voices were joined by many of the locals in the singing of First World War songs.

On 5th December, King George VI arrived in Rumegies; and during the time spent on the Belgian frontier the Battalion was visited by other celebrities, including the Duke of Gloucester,

Allied and German plans before the end of October 1939.

Neville Chamberlain, Winston Churchill, André Maurois and Noel Coward.

Already the newspapers in England were referring to this period as the 'phoney war'; and from the safety of their desk-chairs, journalists began to advise the Generals to get on with the business in hand and taunted Hitler on his seeming reluctance to come to grips with the BEF. Nevertheless, the 'phoney war' dragged on.

In January, the Regiment's 1st-7th, and 8th (Territorial) Battalions embarked with the 48th Division, and the 2nd Battalion was embodied in the same division on 31st January, being brigaded with the 144th. The two Warwickshire TA Battalions had naturally hoped that the 2nd Battalion would move into 143 Brigade when the 5th Northamptonshire Regiment was transferred to 2nd Division, but this was not to be. Instead, the 2nd Battalion found itself numbered with the 5th Gloucesters and the 8th Worcesters, with the 1st Oxfordshire and Buckinghamshire Light Infantry going into 143 Brigade.

It was on 31st January that the 2nd Battalion moved into a mining area at Le Forest and Douai, after an 18½ mile march via Vieux Condé and Coutiches-Flines. The weather was extremely cold, with a frost on the night of 7th/8th February, which was followed by snow. The men were occupied making ready their new positions, which involved digging and concreting on the 1st Corps reserve lines. Visits to the cafés and nightclubs of Lille and Douai were made in leisure-time and there was a welcome ten days' leave in England for most of the troops.

With a break in the weather there was a move on 22nd March to Metz by train. Here, in the Maginot sector, the Battalion was sent forward to relieve the 5th Northamptonshires at the *Ligne de contact*. Patrol activity was lively, with every company having its baptism of shelling. Captain Lynn-Allen and Captain Fisher were with the fighting patrols; and Fisher was awarded the MC for his part in a midnight fight near the German outposts.

A patrol of 'A' Company, under Major Chichester-Constable, met with fire from some houses in Grindorf, with the Major standing in the street, firing at enemy flashes. Private Whitehouse killed a German who was about to fire at Chichester-Constable and was awarded the MM, together with Sergeant Brown, who withdrew with a wounded soldier after hitting two Germans.

On 9th April the Germans invaded Norway with characteristic speed and ruthlessness, and it became obvious that the BEF would soon be involved. The Battalion returned to Le Forest, where it arrived on 23rd April, and where, on 10th May, news was received that Holland and Belgium had been invaded, with their frontiers crossed at several points.

Meanwhile, back in London there had been a Cabinet crisis which had raged during the two preceding days, coming to a head on the evening of the 10th, when Churchill was sworn in as Prime Minister. When this news reached the BEF, there was great excitement, with hopes pitched high.

Also, on 9th May there had been a crisis in Paris, where the Prime Minister (Paul Reynaud) was determined to sack Gamelin, the Allied *Generalissimo,* and to resign if the Cabinet did not agree. Daladier (the Minister of Defence), who held Gamelin in high esteem, blamed the British for what had happened in Norway; in the absence of Cabinet support, Reynaud said: 'I shall have to consider the Cabinet as having resigned', requesting this to be kept secret until the formation of a new Cabinet. Gamelin wrote out his own resignation, but at 1 am on 10th May received news of the 'German columns marching westward', and Reynaud and Gamelin remained at their posts, with the previous day's troubles shelved.

To add to Gamelin's many troubles on the day of the German offensive, between ten and fifteen per cent of the French Army was on leave. Nevertheless, in response to frantic appeals from the Belgians for assistance there was an Allied rush north-eastwards from the Franco-Belgian border to man the main Belgian line of defence along the Dyle and Meuse rivers.

With the rest of 48th Division, which was on Corps reserve, the 2nd Battalion was given notice of a move into Belgium on 10th May and there were frantic attempts to make all companies ready, to the accompaniment of constant air-raid warnings. There was a general feeling of relief that the period of stalemate had ended. The CO (Lieutenant-Colonel Dunn) was away commanding the Brigade in the absence of the Brigadier, who was on leave. He returned on the following day and instructions were given to the adjutant to prepare a letter dealing with billeting in Belgium, care to be taken against spies, the necessity of not allowing troops to accept wine from civilians, the looting of *estaminets* and other related matters. He also made a precis of the various secret letters which had been collecting in the safe for the past few months.

On the 12th, the Commanding Officer gave a talk on the nature of the areas in which the Battalion might find itself in action, with particular reference to Waterloo and the river Dyle. To mark the last night in Le Forest, the sergeants were hosts to the officers at a party where the Commanding Officer revealed his talents as a singer and earned much applause. The adjutant remarked: 'We all had too much beer'. Despite the effects of the previous night's jollity, the adjutant spent the following morning prosecuting at the court martial of a private soldier who had deserted whilst on leave.

Orders to move came from Brigade at 8 pm, and at midnight the troops were moved in RASC lorries, with the Battalion's transport in the convoy. The route into Belgium was through Orchies, Tournai, Enghien and Hal and the road was well marked by pin-prick lights.

On 14th May, Waterbosch was reached, with no one having slept during the night and the MT drivers were tired after driving through the hours of darkness without lights, so a rest was taken in the morning. The only sign of enemy activity was the sight of a German plane which flew along the line of the road. Later in the day, streams of refugees came back from the fighting area and the troops became angry to see old men and women trudging along, weeping as they accompanied the farm carts which were piled high with their belongings. It was a very hot day and streams of cars sped down the road to the residential area of Waterloo, evacuating people and their possessions. 'B' Company was charged with the task of setting up a check-post for the purpose of stopping suspicious cars.

Belgian soldiers began to straggle back, looking dejected and bearing grave news of the German advance and of heavy losses sustained by the Belgian Army. Civilians displayed great interest in the British troops, but the men had been warned to keep away from refugees because of Fifth Column activities. Orders were given for the tearing down of all Pacha Chicory advertisements, because many of these had maps on the reverse side for the use of parachutists and Fifth Columnists.

In the evening the men heard on the radio that a great battle was to take place around Brussels. Indeed, an Army of German tanks had already broken through the French Ninth and Second Armies and was heading for the Channel. On both sides of Dinant, the German XV Armoured Corps broke through the French lines, and in the morning, the greatest blow had fallen around Sedan where the XIX Armoured Corps crossed the Meuse, striking towards the west.

Such were the facts which accounted for the appearance of the refugees and fleeing Belgian soldiers although the gravity of the situation was hidden from the men of the Battalion who, on the next day (15th May) were a mile north of Waterloo when heavy firing was heard. This was presumed to be coming from Charleroi and made to sound nearer by the strong wind. No one imagined that the Germans had crossed the Meuse. During the afternoon a more central situation was found for Battalion HQ in a house next door to the Waterloo Golf Club which had been evacuated by a rich Dutchman. As the troops moved into their fresh quarters they passed farms which had been evacuated. The unmilked cows, whose udders were dreadfully swollen, lowed piteously.

German anti-aircraft fire brought down a British fighter plane which crashed near the golf course, and as the pilot was parachuting to the ground a patrol of 'B' Company was sent out to recover him. Badly shaken and with a leg injury he rested for a time at Battalion HQ, where he was given a welcome drink. Before being taken away he stated that the RAF was fully stretched and faced heavy odds, which was the first indication of how critical the situation was for the RAF.

Before nightfall, news arrived from Brigade that the Germans had crossed the Meuse and broken through the French Moroccan Division's front on the river Dyle. The Battalion was ordered to move up behind them and as the night was very dark and the maps of the area hopelessly out of date with few buildings and no new roads shewn, the journey was difficult. The route lay north of the old battlefield of Waterloo, and to the accompaniment of the sound of distant gunfire the men passed an overturned lorry, some smashed carts and a dead horse. There was a general feeling of suspense as everyone wondered what the next few days would bring.

Ohain Wood was reached at midnight, and as the Battalion arrived at the cross-roads a shell landed about a hundred yards away. Due to the darkness and the difficulty of driving through a 'maze of rides through the wood', several lorries went in different directions – to the displeasure of the CO.

At daybreak on the 16th, the companies were in position in front of the wood, with Battalion HQ in the gamekeeper's house. As rations failed to arrive until 11 am, hardly anyone was able to have breakfast – but one senior officer demonstrated his skills as a poacher, by netting several rabbits. HQ officers fed on Ovaltine which had been discovered in the house, and managed to milk a goat which was in the yard. Overhead, a fierce aerial battle was being fought.

At noon, orders were received to move forward so as to relieve a unit of the Division 'Nord Afrique', but these were cancelled. Instead, the Battalion was ordered to withdraw to a ridge a mile to the rear and hold it so as to allow the 2nd Division to withdraw.

After the adjutant had read the order to the CO, Colonel Dunn said, 'Dick, remember this day, 16th May. It will go down in history as the day on which another classic withdrawal of the British Army began.'

Captain Tomes listened with scepticism, but was later to remember the foresight of the CO.

Later in the day there was a large-scale air-raid on Brussels aerodrome and several fires were seen. Bombs fell uncomfortably close, and the shortage of food led to the looting of eggs from deserted farmhouses.

At midnight there was another move, with the Battalion taking up a position between Waterloo and Waterbosch. In the light of the dawn, Battalion HQ moved to Hoeyk, so as to be able to observe the withdrawal of the companies at 9 am. Several old people were still resident in their homes, preferring to risk the German advance rather than be hustled back with the stream of confused refugees. In mid-morning the companies made their independent ways across country to Breedhout, in order to avoid the possibility of an attack from the air. During this move a private soldier was reported missing and, according to the adjutant, 'never turned up'. Also, a corporal who was in charge of a section of carriers missed his way, and joined up with the 12th Lancers, turning up several days later with news of having been involved in action at Waterloo.

At Hal, the men had not long crossed the canal bridge when they heard the roar from six Stukas which made an attack on a concentration of troops which was about to move along the bottle-neck of the bridge. Many troops and refugees suffered heavy casualties and the men of the Battalion felt themselves fortunate to have escaped the raid. Shortly afterwards, the troops met some men of the Inniskilling Fusiliers who were on their way to delay the enemy's crossing over the canal.

Breedhout was reached at 3 pm, and all companies enjoyed the hot meal which awaited them, and most of the men managed a few hours' sleep. In the early evening a hard-fought air battle took place immediately overhead. Twelve German bombers which had been flying rather low were attacked by four British fighters, who shot down four. One of the two bombers hit by anti-aircraft fire exploded in mid-air. One fighter was shot down.

After visiting Brigade HQ in the next village, the CO held a conference and company commanders were informed that the Battalion was to move about twelve miles to Goeyk for the night. Arriving after dark, the men were billeted in most of the empty farms and houses, with most of the officers being fortunate to obtain beds. Everyone ate a good meal, particularly the officers, who enjoyed wine with their roast chicken – but hopes that the meal would be followed by a good night's rest never materialised when orders arrived for a move out at 1 am, for Herne. The cook's lorries were taken back to 'B' Echelon and all companies were ordered to take as much food and farm produce as possible. This order turned out to be wise, for the cook's lorries were to be missing for the next two days!

At dawn the Battalion was still some distance from Herne, and the convoy came to a halt because of a solid block of vehicles belonging to fleeing civilians. The marching soldiers were ordered on through the fields, but the transport had to be turned around so as to seek a parallel road down a mile-long cart track along which a despatch rider was sent to reconnoitre. A German plane appeared overhead, and for a time, there were fears that the men would be bombed before a move could be made.

Fortunately, all was well from the air – but when the convoy moved off, half of the vehicles (including the carriers and the AA platoon) were held up by a converging convoy belonging to another brigade. Then a carrier broke down and had to be towed along a narrow lane and abandoned, but the vehicle was recovered by Sergeant North later on.

The Battalion was collected together at Herne and there was sufficient time for the men to get some food and drink and a brief rest. The town was thronged with traffic of several divisions and the roads were also crowded with thousands of refugees. Unfortunately, there appeared to be no traffic control in operation and conditions were chaotic.

At 9 am a further move was made. Owing to the maps being out of date together with the many refugees who were on foot, the companies became separated, but managed to link up again later. There were many stragglers and at one time, men of the 7th and 8th Warwicks, Gloucesters and Worcesters were mixed up with the Battalion. Some of these men remained with the Battalion for several days due to the impossibility of finding their units. The marching men became tired and listless under the hot sun, but kept going quite well. But the continual withdrawing was having its effect on morale, in addition to the realisation that the French had cracked badly at some unknown point. Also, many became sombre with the news that the Dutch had capitulated and the realisation that the Belgians were under heavy pressure. Civilians were dismayed to see British troops who had come along these roads returning after but a few days. To their questions there was no reply, for the soldiers were almost as ignorant of the real situation as the civilians. For the first time, the men saw the bodies of old people who had died on their journey and these were buried at the roadside. At every wayside shrine women were praying . . .

The march continued through the hot day and there was little attempt now at keeping step or formation. But not one man fell out, whereas other battalions in the Brigade lost scores of men few of whom ever turned up again. The men of these battalions had not eaten for twenty-four hours, which was considered by many to be due to the inexperience of some TA units in feeding men in the field.

At 4.30 pm the river Dendre was reached and crossed at Papignies. The CO was already waiting to give orders for the men to be checked across the bridge before informing the RE Company which was preparing to blow it up. The tired men worked magnificently unloading trucks, digging positions and making preparations for defence. There was still no sign of 'B' Echelon and the cook's lorries, so the men could not be given a meal. However, Staff Sergeant Lawson organised the brewing of enough tea for everyone.

The Battalion was posted with three companies forward and 'C' Company for patrolling the river bank and counter attack. 'A' Company covered the bridge, for due to the river being canalised the lock gates could not be destroyed and infantry would be able to cross. There were the usual heart-breaking scenes of houses being evacuated and their occupants taking to the roads. The Brigadier visited the CO and imparted the shattering news that the two TA battalions in the Brigade had lost, or mislaid, six companies between them and that another move must be expected in the morning. After having made such good defences it was disappointing to everyone that there was to be another withdrawal, for the men were expecting to fight on the Dendre. But there was nothing else to be done, for the other two battalions could not possibly have fought in their depleted state.

However, although no one knew it at the time, there was a general withdrawal order along the whole line, for the Germans had broken through at Sedan with their armoured divisions. Just before the light faded a large German troop-carrying plane was seen to land about two miles forward of the river, but although there was heavy firing on the left no contact was made with the

ght, Major Cecil Hugh
ichester-Constable, MC,
*ommanding Officer 'A'
ompany, 2nd Battalion,
oyal Warwickshire Regi-
ent, killed in action,
ormhout, 28th May, 1940

low, 'A' Company position
Le Fort Rose Farm looking
direction of German at-
ck.

Officers of the 2nd Battalion, Royal Warwickshire Regiment: *Left to right*: Captain W. Hyde, Captain L. T. Tomes, Captain G. Coulon (French Interpreter), Lt. Col. P. D. W. Dunn, DSO, MC, Captain C. H. Nicolson, Major P. H. W. Hicks, MC, Lt. B. L. Gunnell, Captain A. Crook, RAMC.

enemy. There was an anxious moment when a TA battalion of the Brigade opened up on a 'C' Company patrol on the river bank. Fortunately, there were no casualties – but there were some loud criticisms offered, as they had been previously notified that patrols were being sent out as far as their boundary.

Dawn on the 19th saw another move and, as the vehicles had been sent on earlier, guns, tripods and great coats had to be carried by the men who were tired before the march began. Stragglers increased with every mile and it became necessary for some tripods and greatcoats to be dumped. After about an hour the men were dazed and exhausted and trudged along with no semblance of order, or formation, but with the enemy not far behind, it was impossible for long halts to be made.

The moment of agony came when the embussing point was reached only for the men to be informed that the lorries had been sent to collect part of the 2nd Division. The CO went in his car to find transport to move the men to their destination. However, the march continued. The Adjutant wrote:

The Battalion really did become a rabble now and was a pitiful sight. We got mixed up with other units and refugees. Long halts could not be made and even on short halts we were all apt to fall asleep immediately we sat down.

Lorries caught up with the men at about 2 pm for the purpose of conveying the Battalion to Hollain, and within a short time the troops were amazed to find that they were passing through the familiar town of Tournai. East of the town it was discovered that vehicles of every description were four deep along the road. The traffic jam was such that all vehicles had come to a halt.

As the troops and refugees thronged the street they were alerted by the sound of approaching aircraft, and the town was dive-bombed. Casualties were heavy, and the Medical Officer became exceptionally busy attending to troops and civilians. Many of the men saw German planes with their machine-guns deliberately trained on refugees. This lent credence to the story which had been heard on the previous day concerning an intercepted German message ordering their Air Force to harass refugee columns, in order to increase road congestion.

The convoy was badly knocked about and most of 'C' Company's trucks were wrecked. Some of the drivers were killed and CQMS Sealey was badly wounded. Many of the MT drivers were badly shaken, and one was so seriously affected that on arrival at Battalion HQ, he shot himself. This saddened the officers, with whom he was most popular as he had driven them on many outings to Lille and Douai during the 'phoney war'.

During the raid a travelling circus which was sited in the town sustained damage to some vehicles and several animals broke loose, including a seriously wounded elephant.

Fortunately, casualties inflicted during the raid on the men of the Battalion were light, but the 2nd Gloucesters and the 4th Oxford and Buckingham Light Infantry lost 194 and 48 men, respectively.

Private Arthur Johnson (of the RAOC and attached to the Battalion) had a narrow escape when incendiary bombs landed on the trucks immediately in front and behind, with his own vehicle unharmed. Four men in the AA truck behind his were 'absolutely frizzled to death'.

Johnson also witnessed the lucky escape of Major Hicks when a bullet struck the cigarette case in his left-hand breast pocket, ricocheting. Pulling the cigarette case out of his pocket, he pointed excitedly to the dent and cried, 'Look at that! Just look at that!'

When the attack ceased, George Hall (a signaller of HQ Company) was making his way back to the convoy in the company of a man from Coventry who was the cruellest person Hall had ever met and had, in his opinion, 'joined the Army so as to be able to kill'. Walking through the rubble they noticed a small child, lying wounded and unconscious at the side of the road. The man from Coventry ran towards her and picked her up. As he held her in his arms, he wept. Looking up at the sky, he said, 'Please God, tell me what to do with this.' For one moment Hall felt sure that his companion would put the child out of her misery, which would have been in keeping with his character. However, he placed her on the ground and walked away, weeping.

The air raid in Tournai was the most harrowing experience for the men of the Battalion since arriving in France, and as they climbed aboard their lorries, many felt angry and became impatient to come to grips with the enemy.

The nearby town of Hollain was reached at about 8 am, with everyone feeling tired as they rested in the orchard where they had halted. Although the enemy was close there were no signs of an imminent attack, and many of the troops fell asleep. In his diary, Captain Tomes wrote: 'They could not have moved another yard.'

In the early evening, all companies began to dig in on the western bank of the river Escaut; and though spent in ditches and fields, the night passed quietly with everyone enjoying the first night's sleep in five days.

On the day which had ended, the situation for the Allies had become very critical. North of the river Somme, seven German armed divisions had cut forward to a point which was only about fifty miles from the English Channel. In the morning, members of the French Government, together with the President, the Premier and Marshal Pétain had attended a service in Notre Dame, Paris, petitioning the Almighty for deliverance.

But of such things the sleeping troops at Hollain were unaware.

CHAPTER THREE

Becoming a Real Soldier

What many men of the 2nd Battalion call The Battle of Hollain was but part of the Battle for the Escaut. About four miles north of the 2nd Battalion's position was the Warwickshire's 8th Battalion, at Calonne, with the 1st-7th Warwicks on its rear left-flank. The 2nd Battalion had the 5th Gloucesters on its left, and the 8th Worcesters in the rear.

At Hollain, the men of the Battalion were to face their first, real test with many casualties inflicted and a considerable reduction in the number of troops who would be needed for the later, and sterner conflict.

The Germans were favoured by the situation of the Belgian river town, as Captain Tomes noted:

> The ground was flat by the river, and the slope on which the town stood (which did, in fact, overlook the far bank in a few places) was not adaptable to defence on account of the houses: we could not have stopped the crossing of the river from it. We used it only for a mortar position and observation posts. Each Company had a front of about 700 yards.

One complication was the presence of many civilians who, not unnaturally, were reluctant to leave their homes. Also, precautions had to be taken against fifth columnists and there was evidence of bogus despatch riders and liaison officers. When a man was discovered wandering about the town in a strange and suspicious manner there was some doubt as to whether he was the village idiot, or a fifth columnist; and so he was sent back to Divisional HQ, along with other suspects.

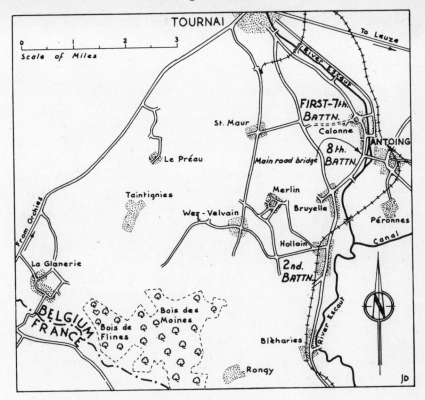

The Battle of Hollain, 1940

Men reported that they were being fired upon by snipers who were secreted in the houses, and it was presumed that this was the work of fifth columnists.

It became obvious that the battle was about to begin when heavy concentrations of Germans were sighted from the observation posts. The mortar platoon opened fire on these, and scored several direct hits. At the same time, there was a fierce attack on 'A' and 'C' Companies' front and the enemy unsuccessfully attempted to cross the river, being repulsed by the bren-gunners and mortars.

'A' and 'C' Companies sustained several casualties, including a couple of sergeants who were badly hurt. Also, some Sappers who were loopholing and performing other work on defences ran back when the shelling began, and several of the men lost their nerve. This resulted in some of the younger soldiers making their way back as far as Battalion HQ.

Obviously, one contributing factor was the removal of the steadying influence of the two wounded sergeants; also, this was the first time the men had been in such intensive action. The Commanding Officer (who was suffering greatly with a stomach ulcer) became annoyed, and armed with his revolver went out with 'a bitter tongue'. The Adjutant decided to accompany him, trusting that his presence would have a calming effect.

When the 'A' and 'C' Company positions were reached, the CO talked to several of the men and sought to explain that things were not as bad as they seemed. That he was possessed of the qualities needed to give an example was manifested when, in full view of the enemy and across open country, he sauntered along. The CO's display of courage had its effect on the men, who became cool and collected.

During the afternoon, heavy shelling was directed at Battalion HQ for a sustained period and it became necessary to accommodate the signals' exchange in the cellar next door, by knocking a hole in the wall. A corner of the house was hit, as was the house which the gunners were using as a forward observation post.

At the height of the shelling, an old man and woman were brought into HQ from the street and with bricks and rubble falling all around them, clung together for safety. Several casualties were reported from the companies, and Sergeant Cruikshanks was accidentally shot dead by one of his own men. This was due to a mistaken password and a nervous trigger-finger.

The Germans suffered heavy casualties in their unsuccessful attempts to cross the river, although a handful managed to land and commenced to fire from the gardens which were in front of 'A' Company.

The Adjutant had several narrow escapes when he was sent to the mortar section, at dusk. His mission was to order them to fire upon some Germans who were concentrated on the bend in the river and thought to be preparing to attempt a crossing when it became dark. As Tomes ran to the yard of the Church where the mortars were situated, the shelling became heavy. On two occasions, when he was rounding a buttress, shells landed where he had been standing the moment before. After climbing a wall, he reached the section and pointed out the target.

On his return to HQ, Tomes discovered that the telephone lines to the companies had several times been cut. The fire was such that after being repaired, the lines lasted an average of ten minutes.

On the next day (21st), the German attack continued during the morning, being concentrated on 'D' Company's front. Owing to the wide front, all companies were well forward and it became impossible to send reserves to 'D' Company. The Germans were in superior numbers and supported by a heavy barrage. The British artillery was far from silent, but it was not possible to use the forward troops because of the real danger of hitting them.

At Battalion HQ messages poured in for assistance, but the CO could only pass them on to Brigade. Once again, the wires were cut by shells and the signallers were kept busy, under heavy fire. Eventually, all messages had to be delivered by runners whose work became arduous and risky. Sergeant Jones delivered messages to Brigade on a motor cycle and was badly cut on the face by fallen wires, but refused medical attention until he was not needed for duty.

News arrived from 'D' Company that the situation was worsening and the Company Commander was killed leading his men into a position from which they could knock out a German machine-gun post. However, 'D' Company held on and the fire from the enemy subsided until mid-day.

The Adjutant discovered that some of the young soldiers in the mortar section were concerned because when they opened fire, retaliatory shells were received. Again, this lack of nerve was due to so many NCOs being lost.

It became necessary for Captain Tomes to arrange for the burial of the many bodies and, together with Sergeant Underhay, was collecting personal effects to send them to relatives. As they walked near the Church they saw the body of Sergeant Cruickshanks, the sight of which upset Underhay for they had been good friends.

Again, 'D' Company was attacked and was in danger of being over-run, which would have led to the enemy moving round and behind. So the CO sent an officer with a party of cooks, batmen and clerks to take up a position to the left-rear of 'A' Company. The idea was to prevent an out-flanking movement. Providentially, the Oxford and Buckinghamshire Light Infantry counter-attacked at the same time and with the help of 'A' Company's covering fire drove the enemy back, and over a dozen prisoners were taken.

The heavy shelling which had been directed at HQ, and all Company HQs, was the result of the presence overhead of a German 'spotter' plane, which had been painted in French colours. This aircraft had been observed to be in attendance on the Battalion on the previous day.

Lance-Corporal Bill Cordrey, of 'B' Company, remembers seeing the 'spotter' plane when he was about to camouflage and disperse his carriers, which were in a farmyard. When the vehicles received direct hits, he appreciated the import of the aircraft's presence. As he looked around, he realised how fortunate he had been to escape injury for in addition to the several wounded men, eight had been killed.

Shortly afterwards, he was again within yards of a bursting shell and lifted from the ground. When he picked himself up, feeling considerably shaken, he saw that the man who had been standing beside him lay dead. A lump of shrapnel had pierced his back. The platoon officer lay on the ground nearby, with shrapnel in his hip. Another soldier had been wounded in the groin.

When the platoon entered Hollain, it was 26 strong. Now, nine of Cordrey's friends were dead and two wounded. He was a regular soldier with eight years' experience, but says that it was at Hollain that he became a 'real soldier'.

In the thick of the day's fighting the (now famous) message was sent out to all units, from GHQ. It read:

News from the south, reassuring. We stand and fight. Tell your men.

The men at Hollain did not need to be told to stand and fight; certainly not those of 'D' Company, who had stood and fought so firmly and valiantly that out of four officers, two were killled and the other two wounded. Only 30 from other ranks remained out of 110.

To add to the Battalion's misfortunes, the Commanding Officer – whose stomach ulcer had burst – only just managed to last out the battle. Tomes says:

> He had just been up to 'D' Company's position and on his return collapsed in the cellar, in great pain. We managed to get him to the Casualty Clearing Station, although he protested strongly – and Hicks took over the command.

The strength of the Battalion was now so depleted as to number only 80–90 men in each company. Tragically, approximately one half of the Battalion had been lost through deaths and casualties. Although the BEF had been in France for about eight months, the real fighting had been numbered in days, during which the fallen and their families had paid dearly for two decades of political ineptitude. In just over two weeks, the situation had deteriorated into widespread collapse.

What had gone wrong?

CHAPTER FOUR

Hindsights

The Allies were not at so much of a disadvantage at the beginning of the war as was once thought to be the case and as the events of May 1940 would lead one to suppose. The French were able to mobilise over 100 Divisions, of which 65 were active; and the Germans had 98 Divisions, of which 52 were active. The British could only mobilise the equivalent of 5 Divisions, but were forming and equipping a Territorial Army of 26 Divisions with plans for these to be increased to 55.

The French had more tanks than the Germans, but most of these were heavily armoured and lacked mobility.

The Germans possessed 1,700 fighter planes and 1,300 bombers, including 380 Stukas. Britain's bomber force numbered 600 planes, with 130 fighters based in France in May 1940. The French were impoverished for aircraft, with 790 fighter planes (including old models) and no bombers capable of undertaking a daylight raid.

The fact that Germany was not overwhelmingly superior in men and equipment led the Generals almost unanimously to advise Hitler that they were not fully prepared for a conflict with France and Great Britain. Also, the French Army was regarded with respect in Europe and even Stalin was to warn Ribbentrop that the French 'still had an army worthy of consideration'. However, the French had been reluctant to adapt to new ideas of warfare particularly as these related to the use of the tank, which was allotted a role secondary to that of the infantry. They also failed to appreciate the offensive use of aircraft – and from these criticisms the British could not be absolved.

It is almost inconceivable that ideas which originated in Great

Britain and France and made public through the writings of Liddell Hart and Charles de Gaulle, were noted without enthusiasm in the countries of their origin but received, taught and practised by German Commanders who perceived the great possibilities of the tank. This led to the creation of Panzer and Panzer-Infantry Units in the employment of which, speed was more important than mere fire-power, together with the use of dive-bombers for 'softening up'.

In addition to being unable to relate to modern methods, the French High Command was divided and confused by intrigue which was not unrelated to the political scene. Between the French and the British there were mutual suspicions, and the lack of co-operation which these sometimes engendered. Added to this was the primitive communications system – particularly that of the French. The disproportionate number of troops under the command of the British Generals meant that they were placed in a subordinate position as this concerned strategy at high level. Furthermore, the commanders and men of the Allied Armies had not been able to profit, as had the Germans, from recent battle experience.

After his brief and successful campaign in Poland, Hitler recommended to his Generals that an early offensive was necessary in the West, maintaining that if he could defeat France, Great Britain would sue for peace. His confidence rested upon recent events which had amply demonstrated the advantage Germany possessed in the ability to exploit the use of modern weapons. He insisted that the attack should be launched in the autumn and that the Maginot line should be outflanked. This implied entry into Belgium before the Allies could strike at the Ruhr.

Brauchitsch (C-in-C) and Halder (Chief of Staff) were opposed to this idea, mainly because of the inferior number of German Divisions. The date fixed for the operation was 12th November, but the weather was so bad that it had to be postponed.

Hitler and Brauchitsch disagreed about the wisdom of the proposed venture and the C-in-C offered his resignation, which was not accepted. The General was told to obey orders. Hitler then settled on the New Year, but the weather again proved unfriendly and the date was put forward for 17th January.

Then occurred on 10th January, an incident which might have sprung from the pages of fiction. Major Hellmuth Reinberger, a liaison officer to General Student (C-in-C of the German Airborne Forces), was making a flight to Bonn when in extremely bad weather his pilot lost his way over the Rhine and was forced to make an emergency landing in Belgium, at Mechelen-sur-Meuse. In Reinberger's possession was a copy of the operational plan of the offensive which was scheduled to take place in the West and soon after landing, he attempted to burn the papers behind a hedge but was disturbed by the Belgians who arrested him. On being taken away for questioning he again sought to burn the papers in a stove, but was caught in the act by his interrogator who was able to recover the papers.

Despite several pages being charred, it was possible for the Belgians to gather that a German offensive was imminent in the West and the plan shewed that an offensive was to be launched on a wide front, between the North Sea and the Moselle. Also, the German Sixth Army was scheduled to cross the Maastricht appendix and advance into Belgium, and parachutists were to capture the bridges on the Meuse, south of Namur.

At first, the Belgians suspected that the whole incident had been devised as a clever ruse de guerre in order to cause them to ask for Allied support – which would have provided Hitler with grounds for an invasion of Belgium. But rumours of an offensive were already reaching the Belgians from Sweden, the Vatican and King Leopold's sister (who was the Italian Crown Prince's wife), together with Intelligence information. Also, it would have been difficult for the landing of the German aircraft to have been faked. Furthermore, warnings had been received from the Belgian Consul in Cologne and the Ambassador in Berlin, that the Germans intended to attack through the Ardennes, together with glider and parachute attacks behind the lines.

The Belgians deduced that the Germans were about to make two deep thrusts – one on the axis from Maastricht to Brussels, and the other from St Vith to Chimay. Such an operation, if successful, would destroy the Belgian and British Armies together with those French forces in the north-east of France. As the captured plan revealed, it was essential that the Germans should capture the Meuse bridges between Namur and Givet.

With their neutrality threatened, the Belgians became anxious and on 11th January, the French and British were informed of the captured plan in a two-page resume. Gamelin was sceptical regarding the contents of the captured plan on the grounds that his Intelligence Staff were ignorant of such preparations as the document revealed. Also, an attack in late winter was unlikely.

On the following day, 13th January, the French Military Attaché in Brussels intimated that the fears of the Belgians were well founded and in the early hours of the 14th, Gamelin was brought from his bed to be informed of an imminent German attack. The British General Ironside was likewise alerted.

It is possible that the news that their operational plan had been captured caused the Germans to revise their strategy, for on 16th January, Hitler decided on a change of plan and the German offensive was postponed. Ironically, the plan would most likely have failed, for the Allied dispositions were placed so as to have been able to absorb the German onrush which in any case would have been over difficult terrain. Manstein was later to observe that until the affair of the captured plan, the German and Allied strategies would have resulted in a head-on clash in central Belgium. But the Allies thought it fit to retain their own plan 'D' which had been conceived by Gamelin. Its execution was that on the German attack, the left flank of the Allied forces would move into Belgium, pushing eastwards so as to counter the German advance which (as in 1914) was anticipated to be made through Belgium. It was known as Plan 'D' after the Belgian river Dyle which would provide a line for the Franco-British troops, but was handicapped by the neutrality of the Belgians and the Dutch. Thus, before a German attack, Allied entry into Belgum was precluded. (See map on page 22)

The retention of Plan 'D' by the Allies suited Hitler's fresh strategy, which had been suggested by Manstein who had foreseen the possibility of a head-on clash, as Belgium was heavily defended at the centre. So he urged the abandonment of the operation formed on the lines of the 1914 Schlieffen Plan and the adoption of his idea for the main assault to be made through the lightly defended

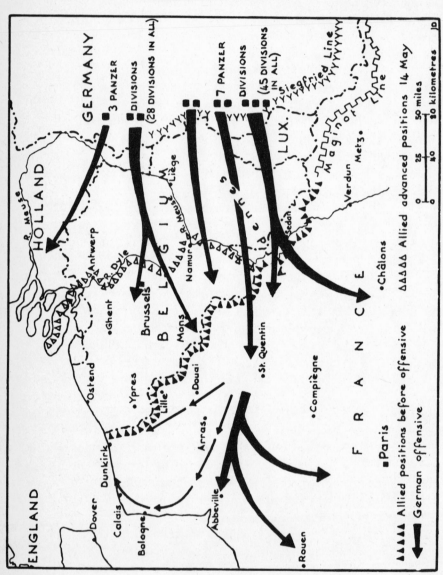

The German attack from 10th May, 1940

Ardennes. The German High Command rejected the Manstein plan, but Hitler (who was concerned about the original plan having been captured by the Belgians) enthusiastically adopted it, incorporating it in his War Directive No 10, dated 18th February 1940.

So, on 10th May the German offensive was launched on Holland and Belgium by von Bock's Army Group B, which consisted of 28 Divisions headed by 3 Panzer Divisions aided by airborne troops and the Luftwaffe. It was anticipated that the vigour of this attack would distract the Allies from the main thrust by von Rundstedt's Army Group A through the Ardennes. Group A consisted of 45 Divisions, spearheaded by no less than 7 Panzer Divisions. The Dutch put up a brave fight, but were compelled to surrender within five days against a German force which, though numerically inferior, was well-equipped and so effectively deployed that German casualties numbered but 180.

As may be expected, the *Leibstandarte* was at the head of the column with the Panzers and crossed the Dutch frontier west of Ventheum, advancing towards Deventer. As the Dutch had blown up the bridge over the river Ijssel the crossing was made at Zutphen, where Sir Philip Sidney was mortally wounded in 1586. On the first day of their remarkable motorised advance, the *Leibstandarte* covered 135 miles.

The SS-troops crashed through Arnhem so as to relieve the German paratroopers who had landed at Dordrecht; and from there, on to Rotterdam and the Hague, where the *Leibstandarte* stayed but one day. The bravery of the Dutch at Rotterdam was such that they threatened to hold up the German advance; and because speed was essential to the success of the whole campaign, the German High Command ordered that the Dutch city should be ruthlessly attacked from the air. Much of Rotterdam was destroyed and the brave Dutch suffered many casualties. It was here that some troops of the *Leibstandarte* were so careless in their enthusiasm as to inflict serious wounds on their own airborne commander, General Student.

From Holland the Germans broke through into Belgium and, as envisaged, lured the most mobile and effective of the Allied forces in the wrong direction into Belgian territory, where the resident Army was already in retreat. The French had fallen into a trap of their own making. Their fixed strategy, derived from a dependence upon the Maginot Line, had left the enemy free to manoeuvre. So as the French and British forces moved into Belgium their rear was open to the enemy's flanking movement through the Ardennes, and as the French had considered the Ardennes to be virtually impassable for tanks the Panzers met with little opposition.

The *Leibstandarte* (together with other Waffen-SS units) did not participate in the fighting on Belgian territory as from the Hague it was transferred south into France with Rundstedt's Armies. The reason for this was that the Panzers who were speeding along at a pace even quicker than had been hoped to the Channel coast, were in need of infantry support so as to clear resistance and occupy territory. So rapid was the German advance that on 16th May, the spearheads were on a line La Capelle-Vervins-Marle-Laon, and it prompted the French Premier to telephone Churchill on the 15th, saying 'we have been defeated'. [1]

Maybe if Gamelin had been prepared to adopt a more flexible strategy the story would have been different, but he stuck to his five-month old plan for a push into Belgium despite the opposition of his colleagues Billotte, Georges and Giraud. Georges, in particular, suggested that it was unwise to be drawn into Holland and Belgium as a defensive manoeuvre in the face of an expected German move which would divert the majority of the available forces and leave room for a main German thrust elsewhere. Also, between November 1939 and April 1940, Intelligence information had suggested that the main German attack would come south of the Meuse, in the direction of Dinant-Sedan. Even prior to the Mechelen episode, Intelligence services had noted a pronounced southward movement of German forces.

On the day after Churchill had received Reynaud's telephone call, the Prime Minister went to Paris accompanied by Generals Dill and Ismay. The meeting was so formal and unrelaxed that everyone stood whilst Gamelin described the grim situation in a five-minute discourse.

[1] Churchill, *The Second World War*, vol. 3, p. 46.

At the conclusion Churchill asked: 'And where is the strategic reserve?', repeating his question in French.

Gamelin shook his head and, to Churchill's surprise and utter dismay, replied: 'There is none.'

Churchill was later to observe that Gamelin's revelation was one of the greatest surprises of his life. It was inconceivable that any commanders with 500 miles of engaged front to defend could have left themselves without a 'mass of manoeuvre'. After some discussion on whether the French Army should dig in Churchill was asked to provide extra fighter cover; and he agreed to order six squadrons of fighters for use in France, in addition to four which already were promised. This gesture meant that only 25 squadrons were left in England for use when required and drew criticism from some historians who have deplored Churchill's generosity.

Meanwhile, Hitler had his own problems which derived from his concern that his armoured divisions were advancing westward at such a pace as to expose the southern flank and Rundstedt expected a counter-offensive by French forces from the Verdun and Châlons-sur-Marne area, northward. Indeed, on 16th May, Rundstedt ordered that all forward operations to the west should be halted – and it was not until the 18th that Hitler could be persuaded to resume the westward advance.

It was on May 18th that the Allied Armies (including the Belgian Army) had completed a withdrawal to the Scheldt. This had taken three days and fortunately the German 6th Army was not in pursuit, as the High Command wished to wait until the Panzers in the south had sprung their trap. This caused General Billotte optimistically, if unjustifiably, to report from his northern Army Group HQ that, 'We are holding everywhere', adding that the Belgian and British withdrawals were proceeding according to plan. However, instead of holding, Billotte should have retreated as quickly as possible south-west into France before being encircled by the Panzers.

On 19th May, Gamelin was sacked by Reynaud and was replaced as C-in-C by Weygand. Already General Gort was considering the possibility of withdrawal towards Dunkirk and in a dispatch written on the 19th he wrote: 'The picture was no longer that of a line bent or temporarily broken, but of a besieged fortress'. [2] But, in response to orders from London, and despite a grave lack of ammunition, Gort endeavoured on 21st May to attack southwards from Arras – and with such success that Rundstedt was moved to describe it as a critical moment. But the British had insufficient armour employed in the counterstroke (a couple of tank battalions, followed by two infantry battalions). Nor did the co-operation of the French materialise as expected.

By 23rd May the German Panzer forces were on the line of the Aa canal, only ten miles from Dunkirk. After much heartsearching Gort took the fateful decision to retreat to the beaches and by the 26th, Belgium was over-run, with the British already having commenced the formation of a bridgehead around Dunkirk, to make a way of escape.

[2] Churchill, *The Second World War*, vol. 3 p. 46.

CHAPTER FIVE

A Place called Wormhout

On the morning of 22nd May, the 2nd Battalion, Royal Warwickshire Regiment was relieved at 3 am by the Oxford and Buckinghamshire Light Infantry and marched from Hollain back to Wez Velvain. Within three hours everybody was asleep, but the much-needed rest was short due to much work which needed to be done. Kit had to be unloaded and vehicles repaired. Lance-Corporal Wright and Private Rose arrived with news that after being captured with PSM Perkins' Platoon they had managed to escape, getting away during the counter-attack. They were able to give valuable information concerning men who were missing and the adjutant spent the rest of the day preparing the casualty report, from which it emerged that a very high proportion of men had been killed or wounded at Hollain.

Wez Velvain was shelled lightly during the day, but there were no casualties. It had been expected that the Battalion would be sent back to the river within the next two days, but orders were received for a move back across the French frontier which was intended to take place later in the day. This grim news came as a surprise. Shortly, there was to be even grimmer news – of German armoured divisions immediately in the rear, with rumours that Calais and Boulogne were threatened. Appreciation of this was difficult, and it was generally felt that a mere armoured column had broken through.

On moving out of Wez Velvain en route for Rumegies, the men marched through the Bois de Ronzy in bright moonlight and were able to see sights which had become familiar during the Battalion's stay on the French side of the frontier from October until February.

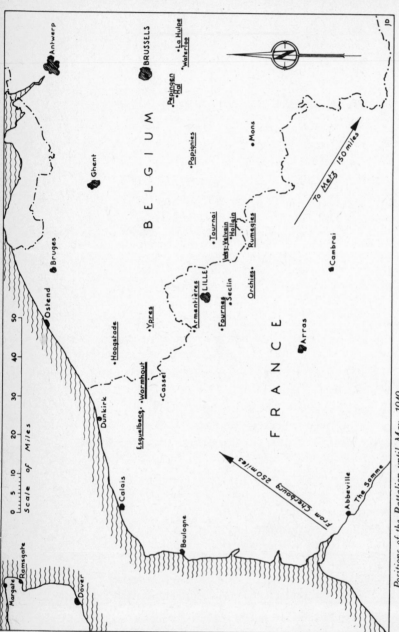

Positions of the Battalion until May, 1940

Cherbourg, 23rd Sept., Rumegies, 5th Oct., Le Forest (Lille) 5th Feb., Metz (by train) 22nd March, Le Forest (Lille) 23rd April, Orchies, Tournai, Hall, May 13th, Waterbosch (near Waterloo) 14th May, Waterloo 16th May, La Hulpe 16th May, Papingem 17th May, Papignies 18th May, Tournai 19th May, Hollain 0800 19th May, Wez Velvain 22nd May, Rumegies 22nd May, Manneuville (Orchies) 24th May, Seclin 25th May, Fournes 25th May, Armentières 25th May, Ypres 25th May, Hoogstade 25th May, Nouveau Monde (3 miles from Wormhout) 25th May, Wormhout 26th May.

The companies were allotted their original posts, which they knew very well after having spent many weeks digging, revetting and concreting in the snow and rain of the winter. That day, 18 men had returned from leave and when the transport had been parked they were sent to reinforce 'D' Company.

May 23rd was a fairly quiet day and necessary work was performed so as to make the Battalion's vehicles and other equipment fit for use. There was more work to be done by the Adjutant on casualty returns, and the CO was occupied with the business of filling positions which had become vacant and deciding who should be promoted. It was a hot day and those who were able to re-explore Rumegies discovered that it was now a ghost town whose houses had been abandoned and looted.

During the afternoon there was much activity in the air. At one time over 40 German bombers flew towards Orchies and Douai, and loud explosions were heard coming from that direction.

In the evening the Battalion was relieved by a French unit and an all-night march began to Orchies, and from there to nearby Manneuville. The small town was jammed with vehicles and packed with French troops and it became necessary to park the transport in farmyards and barns. By dawn, the last vehicle had been hidden and the last company settled in. The much needed rest was quite brief, for at about 7 am a large force of German bombers flew overhead and dropped their bomb-loads along the main Lille road. The adjutant wrote:

> There was little of our AA, and none of our Air Force. We were not to see any of the RAF again, and from now onwards the German planes did what they liked.

In the afternoon news was received that the next leg of the march was to take the men to Herlines and it was before the Battalion reached its objective in the middle of the night that fresh orders were received for a rendezvous to be made at Aubers Ridge, so as to await RASC transport. During this journey further orders came, and the sad Battalion diarist wrote:

25th May. 0100 hrs. At Seclin, orders received for Battalion to proceed direct to Dunkirk. This was a shock.

Few of the men and even the better-informed officers realized the significance of what the Regimental History refers to as 'a long, hot and harassing journey through Armentières and Ypres (which was being bombed) to Poperinghe, where the Battalion halted for three hours to cook a meal and await further orders.'

Eventually, the order to proceed to Dunkirk was modified. Instead the Battalion received instructions to dig in on a perimeter around Wormhout.

Unlike most of the BEF, which already was making for the coast, the 2nd Battalion was to participate in a rearguard action. The importance of the task which was allocated to it is apparent from orders which subsequently were received from the C-in-C:

Hold your present positions at all costs, to the last man and last round. This is essential that a vitally important operation may take place.

Such a task called for soldiers who had been blooded in battle, so it was fortunate that men such as Bill Cordrey had benefited from experiences which he described as having made him a 'real soldier'.

*

Wormhout is a small French town, some 12 miles from Dunkirk. The straight, tree-lined road runs southwards from the coast across flat countryside and connects Wormhout and Cassel, where the road rises steeply. Not far away are places whose names are evocative of the First World War: Ypres, Menin, Poperinghe. Cassel itself was, for a time, the Headquarters of Marshal Foch.

To the west and about 1½ miles away is the town of Esquelbecq, so tiny that most of its houses could be contained within the shadow of its ancient château.

On the morning of 26th May, the fields of Wormhout were wreathed with mist. The weather during the preceding days had been gloriously sunny, and it was said to be the hottest May for many years.

Having marched through the sultry night, the weary troops arrived at 0600 hours.

It was a Sunday, and the inhabitants of the town were asleep in their beds when the men were called to a halt and permitted the luxury of a brief rest. Many fell asleep on the pavement, oblivious of the rain which had just begun to fall.

The companies were allocated defensive positions in and around the town and Battalion HQ was situated in a large house on the north-west corner of the town square, with transport sited in a field behind the house and camouflaged by trees. The First Aid Post was adjacent to HQ.

Although the 2nd Warwicks were responsible for the greater part of the Wormhout perimeter, they were not alone in the area. Ledringhem (about seven miles to the south-west) was the responsibility of the 5th Gloucesters. The 8th Battalion of the Worcestershire Regiment occupied the eastern approaches of Wormhout.

For the residents of the town, the sanctity of the day was marked by the clanging of the bell which called them to Mass and whilst worship was offered up in the Church, the troops began the digging of slit-trenches under the hot sun.

Appropriately, the Sabbath calm was undisturbed by the noise of gunfire and there were few planes overhead: but the civilians were filled with a corporate sense of anxiety as they wondered regarding the significance of the British troops' feverish activity.

The frantic labours of digging-in continued, with food severely rationed, so that all meals were Spartan and hardly appropriate to the labours of the day. Consequently, all ranks were glad to take advantage of the uneventful night.

In Ledringhem, the 5th Glosters (who had been ordered to hold firm for twenty-four hours) were also able to take a night's rest, but this was a little uneasy due to the knowledge that fifth columnists were active in the area.

The Battalion diary for the 27th opens with the observation:

The weather appears to be breaking ... Company commands were complaining bitterly about the inadequacy of map supply, there being only three 1″ maps in the Battalion. Information Officer on motor-cycle to Bergues with object of obtaining some maps from French garrison stationed there. Five 1″ maps of Wormhout and environs brought back.

Gloomy news came early in the morning with the order that 'C' Company was to take up the defence of Esquelbecq, which led to the Battalion's front being further extended.

The other companies were positioned as follows: 'B' Company covered the Esquelbecq road and the Western approaches to Wormhout. 'A' Company was in the centre. 'D' Company overlooked the ground between the roads to Ledringhem and Cassel.

In addition to the troops being thin on the ground, the anti-tank guns were few in number.

Accompanied by the Adjutant, the CO inspected the whole front, visiting every section post and taking stock of the whole area. Each company had a front of about 800 yards. 'A' and two platoons of 'B' Company overlooked a large, open field on their front which, being perfect for tanks, needed to be fairly well protected with anti-tank guns.

It soon became apparent that the overall situation was grave, for several convoys which were passing along the main road had abandoned their vehicles in accordance with orders, the personnel making their way to Dunkirk. Over the distant port was a huge cloud of thick, black smoke and the waves of bombers which passed overhead were obviously making for the same target.

The order from GHQ that the position was to be held 'at all costs and to the last man and the last round' came as corroboration of the grimness of the situation.

The first hint of trouble came at 1400 hours, with the sound of approaching aircraft whose target became frighteningly obvious as the waspish buzz grew into a roaring chorus. Then followed a rapid succession of ear-splitting explosions, which caused the whole town to shudder.

Men whose trenches were fields away, felt the ground vibrate. As the enemy squadron wheeled away, it became apparent that

Wormhout had suffered badly. Hardly a building was undamaged. The streets were littered with debris and civilian casualties became heavy. Fortunately, there were only four casualties in the Battalion, which left the Medical Officer free to assist those who were attending to the injured civilians.

Captain Tomes wrote:

I think this was the worst experience I have ever had and I was definitely more frightened than when dodging shells in Hollain. One could do little but wait for the next bomb and listen to them falling with their high-pitched scream. One felt sickened and exhausted with the clamour and violence and the knowledge that there were none of our planes to take on the enemy bombers. I tried to collect some men for concerted small-arms fire, but that was hopeless. . .

Several old women and children were crouching under a wall, and I herded them into the cellar. One old woman was hit by a piece of falling debris and all the children were too scared almost to move at all. The cellar was not big enough for anyone else.

A few men were able to get into slit-trenches in the park. Harborne, myself, Corporal Cunningham, Lance-Corporal Gerrish and Private Herbert merely stood in the hall and waited. We all tried to remain cool and I think Private Herbert succeeded better than anyone else, making some comical remark after each explosion which shook the house and showered plaster, bricks and glass on to us.

A lorry which was loaded with petrol was within fifty yards of Battalion HQ when a 500 lbs bomb landed alongside. The vehicle was lifted as though by the hand of a giant and blasted horizontally, so as to cause it to crash on the ground about ten yards from the crater. The lorry was undamaged!

Two hours later, it was considered necessary to move Battalion HQ to a slit-trench position about 500 yards away, and it was about this time that a captured enemy order indicated that an attack on Wormhout was being planned for the near future.

The CO and Captain Tomes visited Brigade HQ on the Herzeele

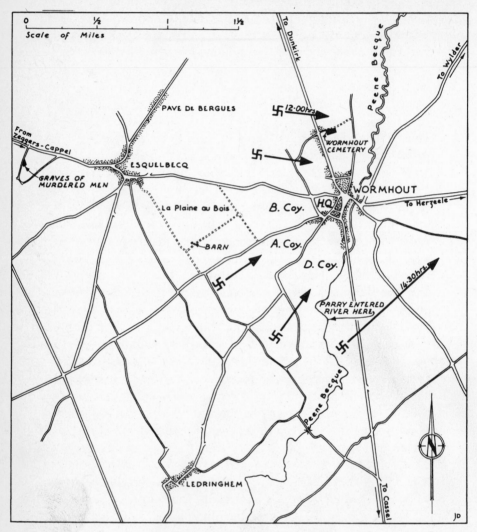

Wormhout – 28th May, 1940

Road, and discovered that they also had been bombed. Pamphlets which had been dropped from a German plane were shewn to Tomes. Written in inferior English, they read:

> British soldiers. Germans surround! You are encircled! German troops invaded Courtrai, Tournai, Vallenciennes. Lillers, Aire, St Omer are occupied. Calais will be taken immediately. Why do you fight further? Do you really believe the nonsense that German kill their prisoners? Come and see yourselves the contrary! The match is finished! A fair enemy will be fairly treated.

At 1600 hrs, came bad news, which was that 'C' Company was to be relieved of the defence of Esquelbecq and sent immediately to Bergues, for the purpose of defending 48th Divisional HQ. But at the same time, some machine-gunners of the 4th Cheshire Regiment arrived to be placed under command. [1]

Company fronts, which already were stretched over the flat countryside, had to be yet further increased. This necessitated the hasty digging of new positions prior to the well-earned rest which was overdue; but hopes of a complete night's sleep evaporated for those at Battalion HQ who knew that only a few miles from the eastern approaches to Wormhout, German troops awaited the order to advance.

That the enemy was active to the immediate south had been apparent during the early evening, when fire was heard from the direction of Ledringhem. In fact, tanks had attacked Arneke, and the 5th Glosters were subject to heavy mortar fire and infantry rushes, but 5 enemy tanks and 4 armoured cars had been put out of action. Dense formations of Germans crossed the railway line, but were shot down in large numbers; and although in greater strength, the Germans were compelled to call off the attack. At 2000 hours, 'A' and 'D' Companies of the Glosters withdrew from Arneke so as to assist their sister companies in the defence of Ledringhem, which was ordered to be held for a further twenty-four hours.

[1] These were Nos. 7 and 9 Platoons of 'D' Company, with 8 Platoon at nearby Wylder.

In Wormhout, the ordinary soldiers such as Bert Evans and Bill Cordrey were not in a position to know more than was afforded by the evidence of the sights around them, or such rumours as proliferated by the hour.

Unlike his comrades, Evans had not had the opportunity of a gradual introduction to the horrors of war for when the Battalion sailed for France, he was under age. Having recently celebrated his 19th birthday, he had been sent out to join the Battalion. Consequently, he had been a member of 'D' Company for no more than a few days, and about the war there was much he failed to comprehend.

As he settled down for the night, he thought of the confusing events which had taken place immediately around him and wondered about the squadrons of bombers which he had seen making their way to Dunkirk. During the day, he had been subjected to his first real war-experience when he was carrying a can of tea back to his trench. As he was about to take a drink, he heard the sudden zooming noise of a plane. Throwing himself to the ground, he lay with his face in the grass and his hands at the back of his neck. Immediately, he heard a 'zip-zip-zip', and a clanging noise. When the plane had roared away, he got up and stooped down for his dixie. It had a bullet-hole in the bottom.

As he lay smoking his last cigarette before closing his eyes, he shuddered with the realisation that the dixie had been lying no more than a couple of feet from his face.

Similar experiences were slipping from the consciousness of many other men in Wormhout whose eyes had closed. But sleep would have been more difficult if they had known that on the day which was ending, Gort had received orders from the War Office 'to evacuate the maximum force possible'[1]. Indeed, nearly 8,000 troops were already being evacuated from Dunkirk.

The recovery of so many thousands more depended upon two German pincer movements. If the jaws closed, the greater part of the BEF, as well as the French First Army, would be doomed. On one flank, the 2nd Battalion was helping to block the path of one

---

[1] Churchill *The Second World War*, vol. 3 p. 7

enemy pincer and the units of 5th Division confronted the other. It was urgently necessary to evacuate as many men as possible before the closure of the German trap.

The final outcome of the war, if not the preservation of Western civilization, depended upon the determination and courage of the men whose function was to delay the closure of the armoured jaws.

So, as the men of the Battalion slept, the Germans were making preparations which were to shorten the night's rest.

CHAPTER SIX

The Attack

With characteristic swiftness the German Panzers sped across France heading for the English Channel, and made such excellent progress that the *Leibstandarte* Regiment was in the St Omer area on 24th May. But, with the Panzers on the line of the Aa canal and bursting to force a crossing, Hitler issued his famous stop-order for the armoured divisions to halt along the boundary of the canal. This order, which was inexplicable even as it was frustrating to the participating Panzer Commanders, was contributory to the successful evacuation of Allied troops from Dunkirk.

With typical bravado Dietrich disregarded the Führer's·order and his Regiment forced a crossing of the canal at Watten, to halt there.

On 26th May, the order was given for the armoured advance to re-commence, and by the 27th the *Leibstandarte* was situated on the line west of Ledringhem–La Cloche–Zegerscappel, from which Dietrich was ordered by his Corps Commander to attack through Wormhout, in the general direction of Dunkirk.

Dietrich ordered the attack to commence on 28th May, at 0500 hours. The battle order was:

On the left: 1st Battalion (Commanding Officer, Kohlroser).
In the middle: 2nd Battalion (Commanding Officer, Schützeck).
In reserve: 3rd Battalion (Commanding Officer, Trabandt).
Tanks of the 10th Panzer Division were in support.

The 3rd Battalion had been engaged in a heavy day's fighting and so the 2nd Battalion was ordered to relieve Trabandt, who was situated about 3 kilometres south-west of Wormhout. The relief was completed at dawn, ready for the attack.

Wormhout was in the battle sector of the 2nd Battalion and, with tanks in support, Schützeck's task was to take the town. He deployed for the attack, as follows:

On the left: Six Company (Company Commander, Anhalt).
In the centre: Five Company (Company Commander, Mohnke).
On the right: Seven Company (Company Commander, Baum).

Each company had the support of a machine-gun platoon from Eight MG Company and the separate units received short, but detailed orders from Dietrich, who was in good mood and confident that any resistance from the British would quickly be overcome.

*

For the British troops, the night's rest was short. The first entry in the War diary for 28th May reads: '0330 to 0430 – stand to.'

The first shells were fired by the Germans at 0500 hours, and landed on the Château and in the nearby wood. Exactly one hour later, 'A' Company was dive-bombed by 15 German planes and there were many casualties. Remorselessly and accurately, the shelling continued. The familiar softening-up process had begun.

The enemy was first sighted at 1000 hours, when Germans were seen to be making for the Dunkirk road north-west of the town, and the stuttering of the 4th Cheshires' machine-guns was immediately heard. Reinforcement of this area became urgently necessary, and so a pioneer platoon was sent up from HQ Company.

Meanwhile, artillery fire was directed at the enemy – but it was not from this direction that the real attack was to come, for 'B' Company saw crowds of refugees approaching on the road from Esquelbecq. Later Intelligence reports mention that some of the enemy were dressed in civilian clothes: and it may be significant that as the refugees were halted at the road-block for interrogation, six German vehicles approached the barrier.

'B' Company promptly attacked the vehicles, which burst into flames. Escaping Germans scrambled into a nearby house and machine-gunned the barrier.

The action began to spread along the whole front, and fields resounded to the crack of small-arms fire. The enemy's shelling was devastatingly accurate and undoubtedly due to the presence overhead of the small reconnaissance aircraft which, since Hollain, had been in constant attendance on the Battalion. On this day it was first sighted at 0900 hours. Tomes recorded that:

It flew backwards and forwards, observing and spotting and we were powerless to stop it. The plane was able to direct mortar fire extremely accurately on to slit-trenches and anti-tank guns, causing large casualties in men and guns before the actual attack came.

Despite the British troops being faced by a force so overwhelmingly superior in numbers, all positions were intact at 1200 hours and casualties at this time were not heavy.

The *Leibstandarte* Regiment, so accustomed to success, was being stretched by men whose courage was frustratingly unyielding; and Otto Baum, who was in the thick of the fight, remarked that 'the resistance offered by the British was very strong'. One of Dietrich's adjutants (Eric Maas) said: 'the fighting started early in the morning and was extremely severe'.

'Sepp' Dietrich stated that the attack which he had ordered to take place early in the morning, 'did not succeed, owing to very strong resistance'. He had not expected such a set-back, and he was puzzled. Nature had endowed him with brute strength allied to quick wits, which had been of advantage in many a brawl. He excelled in the shallows of animal excitement, but floundered in the depths of intelligent appraisal. Wilhelm Bittrich said: 'I once spent an hour and a half trying to explain a situation to "Sepp" Dietrich with the aid of a map. It was quite useless. He understood nothing at all.'[1] In the Röhm *Putsch*, he had not scrupled to participate in the murder of men who had been his best friends, and was sufficiently brash as to refuse even the dreaded Himmler to call him to order.

[1] *The Order of the Death's Head*, p. 405

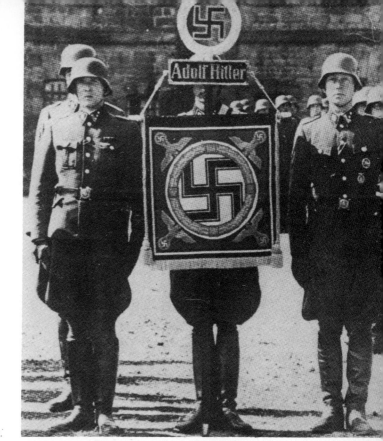

Right. The 2nd pattern 'Adolf Hitler' Standard shown here at the time of its presentation to the Leibstandarte Regiment stationed at Metz, September 1940

Below, Le Fort Rose Farm where some of the Warwicks were held prisoner and which was used as 2nd Battalion HQ.

Sepp Dietrich

The ditch (in front of pole) where Sepp Dietrich hid

He was, if nothing else, a man of action; so, in the middle of the morning, the burly Bavarian Commander pursed his lips and, whistling through his teeth, decided to go over to his 2nd Battalion and investigate the reasons for Schützeck's men having come to a stand-still.

Accompanied by his second adjutant, Hauptsturmführer Wünsche,[2] Dietrich left his 1st Battalion HQ in Esquelbecq by car, making for Wormhout. But after travelling across the flat and open countryside for about a mile, they were hit by a shell from a British anti-tank gun. The car was set ablaze, and the driver died.

Crawling from the car, Dietrich hid in the ditch on the right-hand side of the road. His adjutant crept into a nearby conduit.

Oddly, it was 'Sepp's" 48th birthday!

For hours, he lay still in the swampy ditch and the watchful British were too alert for him to risk the slightest movement. Then came what must have been one of the most frightening moments in Dietrich's life, as he suddenly became aware of a sizzling noise.

Burning waste oil was running into the ditch.

At the risk of calling attention to himself, he tried to beat out the flames and there was one particularly nasty moment when he had to cover his head with mud, in order to survive.

In the nearby conduit, Wünsche became unconscious.

Not until 1700 hours were Dietrich and his adjutant rescued, but not without incident, for an attempt by some men of the *Leibstandarte* to recover their Regimental Commander was checked by British fire.

During the absence of the Commanding Officer, who was presumed to have run into serious difficulties, the SS-troops pressed forward to encouraging cries of '*Heil, Hitler!*', but met with heavy machine-gunning from the Cheshires by way of reply.

It is not unlikely that the unknown fate of 'Sepp' Dietrich helped

[2] Wünsche had been an Aide de Camp to Hitler

[3] The men of the *Leibstandarte* who faced the vicious fire of the Cheshires became so enraged that local opinion in Esquelbecq inclines to the view that this was responsible for the later actions of the SS. A wounded German who was tended by a civilian said that 'everybody talked of revenge'.

to govern the actions of the SS, as these concern the foul deed which was later to be enacted. Undoubtedly, his absence was a blow to the pride of the Führer's favourite Regiment. Also, another incident which would not have been without significance concerned the serious wounding of Sturmbannführer Schützeck, CO of the 2nd Battalion.

At 0900 hours, Schützeck informed his adjutant (Fritz Bütler) that he was going forward to the companies under his command and that any urgent messages could be sent to him by field telephone. Schützeck picked up a runner's rifle, buckled an ammunition pouch to his belt, and left in his car.

At 1000 hours, an order was received at Battalion HQ for an attack to be made on the actual town of Wormhout. Ringing each Company HQ, Bütler was unable to contact the Commanding Officer and, becoming concerned, he decided to walk towards Wormhout in the company of two runners.

As they drew near to the town the sound of small-arms fire was audible, and the three men were puzzled. Meeting some medical orderlies who were proceeding towards the rear, Bütler was told that Wormhout had been under attack for some time and the first houses reached.

Schützeck had obviously ordered the attack on his own initiative.

Bütler moved further into Wormhout and was horrified to learn that Schützeck had been badly wounded and was being taken to the main dressing-station, by car.

He was discovered by Hermann Hasenwinkel, who had been ordered by Otto Baum to go to Battalion HQ to report the breakdown of Seven Company's attack and make request for ambulances, which were needed for the many casualties. The adjutant (Obersturmführer Jürgensen) listened to the report, but made no promises to supply ambulances. Hasenwinkel was dissatisfied, and decided to await the return of Schützeck, but after some time resolved to go into the town.

In the market place he found Schützeck, lying in a car and suffering from serious head injuries. The Germans became very annoyed, because Schützeck's participation in the fighting had inspired his men. Hasenwinkel returned to Battalion HQ and asked again about the ambulances, but was dismissed abruptly by the ill-tempered adjutant who snapped that Seven Company should 'make its own provision for ambulances'.

Meanwhile, as Fritz Bütler made his way back to Battalion HQ he met personnel who were advancing and seeking a new situation for their HQ, so he directed the party to a suitable spot.

The confusion in the Battalion was such that Bütler complained about companies being left behind in the attack. Undoubtedly, the absence of Schützeck, whose courage appears to have exceeded his wisdom, must have contributed to this confusion. The unexpected spirit of the British had created problems for a battalion whose commander was too close to the fighting to be possessed of an objective view of the battle.

As the Germans settled in their new HQ, frantic efforts were made to contact Hauptsturmführer Wilhelm Mohnke, Commander of Five Company (and senior Company Commander), who was to take over the Battalion.

Enraged by the ill-fortune which had attended Dietrich and Schützeck, the SS-troops intensified their attacks and the Warwickshire's old Battalion HQ (which was vacated on the previous day) sustained heavy damage. Around the new HQ, which was at the far end of the park, personnel continued to dig trenches.

Throughout the morning the signals section was a hive of activity, with Privates Reginald West and White kept busy as they maintained contact with Brigade HQ and the companies.

During a lull between messages West sensed that activity was being stepped up, and he began to fear that in a short time his lines would be severed. Looking at the rifle which was propped up in the ditch which served as a signals 'office', he wondered how he would be able to defend himself when the occasion arose – for there was no ammunition.

That the situation regarding ammunition was general, emerges from the terse note in the Battalion diary, timed at 1300 hours: 'Shortage of small-arms ammunition.'

Unfortunately, the shortage was not confined to small-arms am-

munition, as Alf Tombs had already discovered. With him in their
position behind a hedge were Sergeant Moore, George Hall and
about six others. For their 3″ mortar there was no ammunition, and
as the enemy's fire intensified, they could only lie still; and with
their nearest neighbours hundreds of yards away, they suffered the
feeling of isolation which is the psychological enemy of every
front-line soldier.

Their anxieties were shared by Bill Cordrey in his 'B' Company
position, whose own words convey realism: 'I could see movements
from other sections, but that uneasy feeling began to return. One
thing in our favour was that we had a wonderful field of fire.
Whoever had sited that slit-trench, had done a good job.

'Suddenly, things began to happen. Over to my left, I could hear
small-arms fire and the sound of mortars. I had just made up my
mind to go for a quick look, when Ginger shouted: "Look, Corporal! Right in front!" And there, about seven or eight hundred
yards away and coming towards us, was a long line of figures.
Sticking the sights up to 800, I fired a long burst – and within
seconds, the sections on my right joined in. We must have been
scoring hits, because gradually the line started to break up into
small groups. The action had become fairly general and it wasn't
long before we were getting our fair share of Jerry shells.

'After a while, things began to quieten down, but over to the left,
things were really hotting up. We weren't to be ignored for long!
Then, the section on our right started firing. I couldn't see what
they were having a go at, and I spotted half-a-dozen small groups
making towards us.

'It seems that Jerry had learnt a lesson from the first attack and
was trying different tactics. But there was no cover for them, and
we had them pinned down before they had moved a hundred yards.
They seemed to advance in small rushes, but at last they gave it up
as a bad job. They must have been losing far too many men but I
must admit, they had guts.

'A lull occurred in the fighting, and I told Ginger to take over the
Bren – but not to fire unless he had a good target. At the rate we
had been using ammunition, it wouldn't last long.

'I was wondering how the other lads were faring when, not more than a couple of inches from my head, the parapet was being cut as if with a knife. I heard the rat-tat-tat of an automatic weapon and came down from the parapet, like a scalded cat! I'd had a few lucky escapes at Hollain, but this was too near.

'The thought crossed my mind that Jerry had broken through on a flank and got behind us, but the more I thought about it, the more sure I became that the fire had come from our own guns. Grabbing a rifle, I told Clancy to take over. I was going to find out what the bloody hell was happening! I ran across the road, when a bullet zipped past me. A couple of seconds later, another! A sniper was having a go at me.

'I dived into the ditch which ran alongside the road and half-crawled, half-stumbled along. A few hundred yards away I could see men moving about, right in front. I guessed I was near the village. Actually, I must have reached Battalion HQ.

'Just as I was going over to one of the men I bumped into Major Hicks, the acting CO. I told him what had happened, and asked if he thought we had been placed too far forward so as to be caught in our own fire. He replied that he didn't think so, adding that he would have a check made. He asked about the situation in our part of the line, and as we were talking, I couldn't help thinking that he was a very worried man. As I left, he assured me that he would get in touch with me and so I made my way back. Little did I realize that I would not see him again.

'I arrived back at the trench to find that all had been quiet, although Clancy said that a few minutes before, he thought he had heard a rumble but was not able to see anything.

'Ginger wanted to know if I had brought any food back, and I told him that some was coming up in about an hour's time. It was a lie, but there was no sense in letting him know how uneasy I was getting.

'Suddenly, "Titch", who was on look-out, shouted, "Quick, Corporal, come and have a look at this!"

'Even before I looked over the parapet, I knew what it was. Subconsciously, I had been listening to a low hum, and the penny dropped.

'Tanks!

'Sure enough, there they were, about 700 yards away and making towards us in an extended line. I made a dive for the Boyes anti-tank rifle. Ten bloody rounds! What the hell good was that?

'Everybody was opening up now, and the sections on my right were really letting go. As I heard the snap of an anti-tank gun, I began to wish that we had more of these.

'Sticking the barrel of the Boyes over the parapet, I picked out the most central tank and decided to let him have the full ten rounds. Now, I'm no Bisley champion shot, but at that distance I didn't reckon to miss. The previous year, I had been on an anti-tank rifle course and our instructor had told us that these .505 bullets would penetrate armour, spin around the inside of a tank, fragment, and kill all the occupants.

'What a joke! That bloody tank never faltered, and I knew I was hitting it.

'The situation was getting really hot. We were being plastered with shells and automatic fire. What to do? Get out, while there was still chance? Or keep on with our pea-shooter of a Bren, and get massacred?

'Every nerve in me was screaming, "Get out! Don't be a bloody fool, you've done your share". But I was more scared of running than of staying put! I could hear Ginger, cussing like hell. The Bren had jammed, and he had bruised his thumb.

'This was it! Time to go!

'Suddenly, Clancy said: "Quick, Bill! Look! They're turning!" I took a quick look, and sure enough, the whole line had made a half-left incline – and the extreme right flank was going to miss us by at least a couple of hundred yards.

'I couldn't believe my eyes. Another few minutes, and it would have been curtains for us. As the tanks moved away, I expected to see the infantry following up behind them. But it was all clear.

'Years later, I met Corporal Thomas who had been in the next trench to us. He told me that a tank went right over his trench, and everyone was killed except himself. But he lost both legs. He also said that the whole of the line to his right, was wiped out.

'Except for a few bursts of gunfire to our left, everything had gone quiet. In my own mind, I was certain we were in a pretty bad fix.

Eventually, I decided to send Clancy out, to have a scout around. I told him to try and find Company HQ, but not to be away for long. I had a feeling that he wouldn't find anything, and I wanted to get out as soon as possible.'

The tanks which had moved away from Cordrey's position were pushing their way round to the right of 'B' Company. Lieutenant Dunwell's platoon put up a spirited fight, sustaining heavy casualties.

Lance-Corporal W. H. Handyside is mentioned in the 'B' Company diary as having 'fought a gallant battle'. Though wounded, he fired his Bren gun unaided, and hung on until he was completely isolated and without ammunition. Afterwards, he withdrew to Company HQ with his gun, took several wounded men with him, and assumed command of the situation by posting two Lance-Corporals at the rear of Company HQ.

The line to Brigade HQ was severed, and a message to Battalion HQ which read: 'Tanks shelling and mortaring' failed to arrive. Lieutenant Dunwell and Corporal Handyside[4] were killed in the fighting. Two or three attempts were made to contact the remainder of the Company, and the CSM, CQMS, 2 cooks, one stretcher-bearer, a batman, 5 truck drivers and one signaller moved forward to the hedge. The 'B' Company diary states that here they 'lay-up for five hours'.

At 1430 hours, the Battalion diarist wrote: 'The battle raging furiously and tanks reported advancing down the road from Esquelbecq'.

Already the people of Wormhout had left their houses, many of which were ablaze. The whole neighbourhood was in the throes of the desperate struggle, but the lightly and sparingly-armed British defended their positions with vigour. Outnumbered by the better-equipped and well-supported SS-infantry, they exploited the open terrain so as to encourage the Germans to enter the trap areas which had been prepared. Their bravery was such that the war diary of the attacking German XIX Corps, stated:

---

[1] The headstone on Handyside's grave in Wormhout cemetery incorrectly states that he died on 27th May, thus making it appear that he did not participate in the fighting.

The Corps Commander is not counting on any success from the attack and is of the opinion that further useless sacrifice must be avoided after the severe casualties which the 3rd Armoured Regiment has suffered.

The German diary entry was timed at 1430 hours, but with typical nonchalance the *Leibstandarte* Regiment persisted with the attack and continued to employ its supporting armour.

Of the incidents of heroism in the face of the armoured advance, none is more poignant and arresting than the one recorded of Major C. Chichester-Constable, MC, who was 47 years of age, [5] and in command of 'A' Company. During the First World War, he was captured in 1914 and remained a prisoner for over four years, displaying such pluck and endurance in attempting to escape that he was awarded the Military Cross. He was extremely popular with his men, who esteemed him for his courage and imperturbability. His last courageous act can be told in a few words. He was seen walking towards the approaching enemy tanks, alone . . . and with a pistol in his hand. He died in the arms of an SS-soldier and fellow Roman Catholic, who was himself killed on the following day. [6]

On the day of the Major's death, his brother (Brigadier R.C. Chichester-Constable, DSO) distinguished himself at nearby Bergues and was awarded a bar to his DSO. By a 'masterly handling of his Brigade', he launched a counter-attack and flung the Germans back into the marsh. From that defeat the Germans attacking Bergues never recovered, and only advanced after the last of the British had left Dunkirk.

---

[5] The headstone on his grave in Wormhout Cemetery incorrectly states his age as 45 years.

[6] In 1946, the *Daily Telegraph* published an article asking Chichester-Constable's next-of-kin to contact them. Eventually, his uncle received a package from Munich which had been sent by the father of the German soldier who had written home the night before he was killed. Letters from the Major to his grandfather were included.

CHAPTER SEVEN

The Fortunes of War

Bert Evans peered cautiously over the parapet of his trench. It was early afternoon, and 'D' Company's position seemed to be attracting the undivided attention of the enemy's mortars, and Evans had been subjected to several showers of earth. A quick glance told him that tracts of land which had recently been unmarked, were now badly scored and pot-holed. It seemed inevitable that within seconds his trench would be hit, and Evans became anxious.

Then followed a period of respite, during which he felt emboldened to straighten himself so as to take a careful look around – and then he caught sight of the German tanks. They were the first he had seen in action and he felt a curious sense of detachment as he watched them trundling nearer. There were about six of them and when he first caught sight of them, they were quite close together. Then they fanned out – and as this happened, he noticed the infantrymen following up.

In an instant, he decided that it was essential to put as much distance as he could between himself and the fearsome-looking vehicles, which seemed to be bouncing along. There was only one direction in which he could go, and that was to the rear.

As he ran, he could hear them coming on and seeing a farmhouse, felt tempted to run into it, but quickly realized the uselessness of the building as a hiding place. As he sensed the gap behind him to be narrowing, he suddenly noticed that the river was immediately ahead.

He was trapped.

Others who had reached the bank jumped into the water – but Evans could not swim and as he reached the water's edge, he turn-

71

ed around. With his heart thumping in his chest, he saw that there
was no escape from the eight or nine Germans who had caught up
with him. As he put up his hands, he noticed that they were
SS-soldiers and caught sight of the name Adolf Hitler on their
sleeves. 'They're not just Germans' he said to himself, 'but bloody
Nazis!'

Within a few minutes he was joined to another party, which
numbered about 50 men of 'D' Company, whose position had been
in the battle sector of the *Leibstandarte*'s Seven Company.

Some of the 'D' Company prisoners had been taken by the German 2nd Platoon of Seven Company. That the human trophies
were hard-won is apparent from the story of the Platoon leader,
SS-Untersturmführer Heinrichs.

The Untersturmführer had heard that the British were very active in the area of his objective, and so led his men with caution as
they approached the outskirts of Wormhout. Proceeding on the
left-hand side of the road which led into the town, the Germans
passed one or two buildings when Heinrichs realized that it was
necessary to cross the road. As he motioned for his men to follow,
the British opened with a savage fusillade of rifle fire. Heinrichs
screamed for his men to run for the cover afforded by the front gardens of the houses and with corporate alacrity, they scrambled over
the low wall. Surprised by the suddenness of the attack and
breathless from their exertions, they crouched behind the wall. Just
as the Untersturmführer was making up his mind to advance under
cover of the houses, he heard the shout of a familiar voice.

It was Otto Baum!

Impatient that his men should keep up with the attack, Baum
barked at Heinrichs to move on with half his men forthwith.

Cursing the unwelcome attentions of the British and the unflagging persistence of Baum, the young SS-Officer carried out the order
and, with six men, advanced along the left-hand side of the street.
As they dodged from the cover of one house to the next, the Germans met an increasing spate of fire and Heinrichs' spirits rose
when he was joined by a platoon of Five Company.

It seemed that the British were having to contend with opposition which, to Heinrichs was unseen, and gradually the British fire

petered out. Eager for the kill, the Germans quickened their pace and captured several men, some of whom were hiding in the houses.

These were joined to the party which included Evans, who witnessed an incident whose importance is such that it needs to be told in his words:

'As we were being marched along, feeling miserable at having been captured, we approached a pill-box. One of our chaps who was still at large must have been just behind it, because he was hidden from us. Anyway, as a tank came past the pill-box, he lobbed a hand grenade into the open turret. It exploded inside with such a loud noise that I was reminded of how, as kids, we used to put bangers into tin cans so as to try and make a louder bang. I reckon the tank crew must have been killed, outright.

'This made the Germans very angry and they immediately began to shout at us, and push us around. Not that the chap who had thrown the grenade had been in our party, for he had not yet been captured. What happened to him, I can only guess.

'After a short time we were halted in front of a shed, where there were other prisoners lined up. I could not recognise any of them. They might have been from the Cheshire Regiment. Anyway, there were about fifteen of them: and as they stood there, the guards who were in charge of them opened up with automatic fire.

'They killed the lot. I shall never forget seeing them fall down, just like rag dolls.

'To this day, I can never understand why we were not shot along with them. I can only think that our guards belonged to a different company, or something like that. But what I do remember, very clearly, was thinking that something nasty seemed to be afoot.

'Anyway, we were moved off again.'

Feeling apprehensive, the 'D' Company prisoners were pushed across a footbridge and along a footpath, on to the main road from Cassel. Along the road they were taken for about forty yards in the direction of Wormhout, where they were lined up in front of a house which was on the right-hand side of the road.

They were searched in an extremely rough manner. Captain Lynn-Allen had a hand-grenade, a revolver, a ring and the contents of his pocket confiscated. During this search, some of the men were stripped to the waist. Identity discs were removed from all prisoners.

Shortly to be joined to the group was Gunner Richard Parry, whose experiences prior to capture were most eventful.

His Battery (242: 69th Medium Regiment, Royal Artillery) was making for Dunkirk, and as the convoy approached Wormhout from the south, it was ambushed in the neighbourhood of the Peene Becque.

When the convoy came under fire, Parry was sitting in a Scammel truck with a goatling in his arms. As he stroked the little animal, Parry heard the sound of gunfire being directed at his truck. This was coming from an approaching tank, accompanied by a small group of infantry.

Obeying orders, the occupants of the truck scattered and Parry ran into a nearby warehouse on the bank of the river. Breathless, he peered through a window in the building and gazed at the water. He was a capable swimmer and felt sure that if he followed the river in the right direction, he could swim to the coast.

Taking off his boots, he tied them together and hung them around his neck. Creeping to the water's edge, he looked each way before getting into the water. As quietly as possible, he swam under cover of the bank.

After about a mile-and-a-half, it occurred to him that he might be going in the wrong direction and when he saw a row of houses, he decided to find out if there was some means of discovering his whereabouts. Clambering up the bank of the river, he made his way into the nearest house. His intent was to find a map, and he was heartened when he entered a room which contained shelves of books. Feeling certain that there would be a map in the room, he searched carefully and came across the very thing he was seeking – but his pleasure was immediately diminished when he saw that it was a map of the south of France. Bitterly disappointed, he decided to leave the house by the front door and when he stepped outside, he was alarmed to see a party of SS-troops standing on his side of the road, and about fifty yards away.

As he cursed his luck, two Germans hurried towards him and as they approached they motioned with their rifles for him to raise his arms. They then took him across the road and searched him. His steel helmet, pay-book and other personal belongings were taken from him, whereupon he was accompanied for a short distance to a wooden-fronted building. On the pavement was a group of prisoners. This was the party which included Bert Evans.

For what Parry estimates as being a quarter of an hour, the men were compelled to hold up their tired and drooping arms until another German appeared. He had emerged from the Estaminet St Hubert, which was across the road, and appeared to be an officer. Rather angrily, he gave the prisoners permission to rest their arms, which came as a welcome command.

*

Alf Tombs was numbered with the unhappy group, and prior to capture had been with a small party of 'D' Company men which included George Hall. Captain Lynn-Allen had instructed them to make their way to Battalion HQ, for the purpose of collecting ammunition. Two men who had originally been sent on the same mission had not returned, which led Tombs to suppose that their task was extremely hazardous.

The intensity of the enemy's fire made it necessary for the men to take advantage of such cover as there was; and at one point, progress could only be made along a ditch. It was as they were crawling through the thin mud, and in single file, that a most distressing incident took place.

The man in front of Tombs had neglected to replace the safety-catch of his rifle, and the trigger was caught in a twig. With a disturbing report, the weapon went off – and a Private Gould, who was immediately in front of the rifle, received the bullet in his back. Gould slumped in the mud, unconscious. It was impossible to take Gould with them, so the men laid him on a bank, near a gate. However, the enemy's fire meant that further advance would have been suicidal and the men decided to take up their position.

Within minutes, they were surprised to see a despatch rider staggering towards them. Having made his way through a hail of bullets, he was suffering from a severe wound in the stomach; and as he was carrying a message, the men (who, in any case, could not accomplish their mission) took him to Captain Lynn-Allen.

On the departure of the despatch-rider, Lynn-Allen turned to the men and said, 'My God! There was no need for the poor chap to have come. I shall see that he is mentioned in despatches.' He then added, 'This is the end. But you have no need to be ashamed, for you have fought well.'

Within a short time enemy tanks appeared and the men were taken prisoner. On the way, they passed the place where Gould had been left and a German went over to him, pointed his rifle at the wounded man's head, and fired.

The bewildered prisoners were marched for some distance until they came to a farm building, and were ordered to line up against a wall. For one awful moment the thought occurred to them that they were about to be shot when a machine-gun was placed on the ground, its muzzle facing them. But their fears were dispelled by a welcome order to move off.

On the way, they came across the gruesome sight of three trucks: and by the side of one vehicle, the charred bodies of British soldiers. To add to their misery there was a heavy shower of rain, and they became soaked. Eventually, they arrived at the point where they were joined to the main party of 'D' Company prisoners and with their uniforms still sodden, they were compelled to hold up their arms.

The party was then marched in the direction of the Church, which had not escaped damage, and they turned left. Passing a line of houses they saw two or three soldiers who had been hiding in doorways. These were arrested and joined to the pathetic column.

Moving through the town they were compelled to watch the houses burn and this to the sadistic satisfaction of their guards, who motioned and grinned.

Bearing left of the town, they reached the German Battalion HQ, which was situated in an open field on the right of the road leading from Wormhout. Here they were joined by a party of between 30 and 40 prisoners, mostly of 'A' Company, but including some Cheshires and one or two Gunners.

The time would be about 1630 hours, and Hauptsturmführer

Wilhelm Mohnke had not long taken command of the *Leibstandarte's* 2nd Battalion although there is no evidence that he either knew of or condoned the atrocities which were to follow.

Rottenführer Oskar Schauff had helped to bring in some of the 'D' Company prisoners and together with other SS-guards, halted outside the Battalion HQ for instructions concerning the disposal of the captives.

As he waited, he was astounded to witness a *Leibstandarte* senior officer – emerge from Battalion HQ stride up to Untersturmführer Heinrichs and angrily reprimand him.

Richard Parry remembered the incident and afterwards described 'an SS-officer who wore a soft, peaked cap and seemed a "big noise". He was giving orders to his subordinates and, from his gestures, about ourselves. He was raving blue murder! One of the chaps who understood German, said: "My God! They're taking no prisoners". The officer who was doing all the shouting was still there when we moved off.'

As the prisoners began the last leg of their journey, Charles Daley, of 'A' Company, was feeling weak from the bullet wound in his shoulder which he sustained shortly after his capture when a German who was armed with a revolver shouted '*Engländer Schwein!*', and for no apparent reason. In his rage the German promptly shot him. Like others in the party, Daley found the next stage of the journey almost unendurable, because for a distance of over a mile the prisoners were marched at double-time. This was verified by the SS-guard who was later to state: 'We ran across the fields'.

Some unfortunate men who could not maintain the pace of the rest, were cruelly treated: and those guards who were slightly less sadistic than their more brutal comrades, merely kicked those prisoners whose condition compelled them to falter.

Richard Parry was assisting a wounded comrade to maintain the pace of the others. He became tired from the added weight, and was desperately anxious to slow down – but on seeing one of the men being bayonetted, felt particularly keen to keep up.

Bert Evans was flagging before the forced march over uneven

ground was completed. His will to keep going was provoked only by the cruelties inflicted on the stragglers. One man who had dropped to his hands and knees in an attempt to crawl along, was stabbed in the chest by a bayonet. Another was clubbed about the head with the butt-end of a rifle.

As the party neared its destination – which was on the edge of a large field in *la Plaine au Bois* – Reginald West had yet to join it.

The story of his capture commenced in HQ Signals section where during the morning the signals traffic had been quite heavy. One long message was addressed to all battalion commanders, and concerned the withdrawal to the beaches. It was headed: 'For the Information only' of the Battalion, but West hoped that this would prove to be wrong as he guessed that the situation in Wormhout was hopeless.

In the early afternoon he was asked to send a message to 'A' Company, but the line was dead. Picking up a reel of cable, West was joined by Captain D. Padfield (whose promotion from Lieutenant had been notified on that day). Together, they set off for 'A' Company, but their progress was slow because the enemy was close at hand. In between short bursts of speed they were compelled to take cover. After about ten minutes, they were alarmed to see a German tank followed by SS-infantry, approaching from 'A' Company's position. Escape was impossible, and the two men were soon surrounded by a small group of Germans.

Captain Padfield's reaction amazed West, even as it must have surprised the Germans, for he quickly pulled out his pistol. The response was immediate, and Padfield's body was riddled with bullets.

West looked down and saw the blood seeping through the dead officer's uniform. Angrily, he clenched his fists. He was a fair boxer and in normal circumstances would have used his skill to the detriment of the Captain's murderers, but he was quickly overpowered by two Germans who searched him for weapons.

As the men in the forward companies felt the grip of the enemy to tighten, so the anxieties of the staff at Battalion HQ multiplied. Communication with the companies became spasmodic as lines

were severed, repaired and shattered once more. Such information
as was received was dependent upon those who came in with
messages, or requests for ammunition and materials. Though the
morale of those who came back was remarkably high, the news they
brought became more grave.

That there was a crisis in the whole sector became clear as news
was received from other units. At Ledringhem, the 5th Glosters had
been subject to intense fire; and in one attack the Germans entered
the town, but were driven out at the point of the bayonet . . .

Also, men from other sectors began to trickle in, and Tomes
wrote:

A French soldier with a gaping wound in his shoulder turned up
from somewhere. A very shaken AA Lieutenant turned up, having lost his battery and himself.

Movement in the open became increasingly dangerous, and two
men who had brought a message in to Battalion HQ returned to
their companies through a hail of shells. However, men of all ranks
displayed an amazing optimism until the end. One man brought a
message from 'B' Company to Battalion HQ and was described by
Tomes as being 'very excited and in tremendous fighting spirit, and
said that he wasn't going to let any "bloody Jerries" get past him.
He went up the road with a happy grin.'

Only one carrier remained for use and was sent backwards and
forwards, with ammunition.

As the enemy's shelling increased, the noise became loud and
constant. Such reports as came in at 1415 were ominous and told of
tanks which were already attacking, or preparing to attack, with
accompanying infantrymen in large numbers.

The Adjutant wrote:

It became obvious that we could not stop a tank attack, and
would be merely over-run. After all, we were but a few scattered
infantry posts, without our mortars, both guns of which had been
destroyed, and no carriers, very inadequate artillery support –

and no air, or armoured support whatsoever. But the Battalion had at any rate, delayed the advance.

Sometime before mid-afternoon it became obvious to the Commanding Officer that the end was near. A message to that effect was sent to Brigade HQ. There being no signals contact, its delivery bordered on the miraculous as Sergeant Jones drove his motor-cycle through heavy bursts of fire, his body stretched over the handlebars.

Headquarters was now completely isolated from the companies, with the result that no further messages were received or delivered and for the last stand, all available men were actively employed, being placed along hedges and ditches in ones and twos.

The ominous lull in the firing told its own quiet message that all company positions were over-run. The imminent approach of the enemy was heralded by a sudden loud explosion which broke the silence: and as the position of the defenders was sighted, so the storm became a hurricane which glowed intermittently with the tracer-bullets.

At around 1415 hours, armoured cars approached on the left of HQ and paused preparatory to firing from behind a hedge, some two hundred yards away. In front, a farm which housed the Bren section was in flames.

The adjutant's account of his involvement in the fighting is descriptive:

'I saw a man with an anti-tank rifle. I don't know where he had come from. I told him to follow me, and started off up the road towards the armoured cars, which were behind the hedge. He couldn't see where they were, so I took the anti-tank rifle and lay down in the middle of the road, covered by a derelict truck.

'I fired two of the remaining three rounds. I couldn't see whether they had any effect. I was feeling curiously exhilarated now, and still had a rifle and fifty rounds which I had taken off a carrier. It had belonged to one of the crew, who had been killed.

'After placing the man with the anti-tank rifle in position, I got behind a hedge and fired practically the whole bandolierful at the turrets of the armoured cars (one became ditched) and at various vehicles and motor-cycles coming along the road.

'Hicks sent up Private Fahy, and we fired at these for several minutes. My rifle became almost too hot to hold, and I heard Hicks shouting at me to come back. Fahy and I ran back along the road, which seemed alive with splattering bullets and tracer. The direction of these made me look left, and I saw two tanks coming towards us across the field. They must have wiped out the Intelligence Section, who were at that corner.'

These events are expanded by the Battalion's War Diary in an entry timed at 1430:

Tanks reported advancing down road from Esquelbecq. Distance about 100 yards. Remainder of Battalion HQ and Headquarters Company, Majors Hicks and Harborne, Adjutant and Intelligence Officer, now joined by 2nd Lieutenant J. W. Tomes, with signallers, intelligence, MT drivers and others, returned in single file towards Château, with the exception of Orderly Room clerks, two or three Intelligence Section, who remained behind in slit trench and fired at an advancing tank. Tank passed down towards village. Battle raging furiously. Many casualties. RSM presumed killed. Party with CO take up positions in slit trenches in garden near old Battalion HQ. The air was full of bullets. Tank on Esquelbecq road, and tanks advancing across country, all firing vigorously.

During this stern fighting, Captain Tomes was hit by a bullet which struck his helmet and he fell to the ground. Discovered by stretcher-bearers, he was taken to the First-Aid Post where the Medical Officer was in the cellar, looking after the wounded.

The Commanding Officer realized that further resistance was impossible and that it was vitally necessary to find some way out, for the circle of steel was closing remorselessly.

Accordingly, Major Harborne was detailed to explore the possibility of escape at the back of the garden, but within minutes he returned to report that such a move would be disastrous. The diary continues: 'He then took up a rifle and went out with one private soldier to fire at a tank – and was shot through the head.'

The entry was timed at 1445 hours, and makes mention of a violent thunderstorm which was raging, with the rain pouring down.

Fortunately, a sergeant discovered a means of escape, and the diary adds: 'CO led party away from Château garden with 2nd Lieutenant Tomes and about 65 other ranks across the Dunkirk road to Brigade HQ . . . and thence to Wylder.'

Also escaping from the park was 2nd Lieutenant Vaudrey, together with eighteen men of HQ Company. Eluding capture, the party reached the Dunkirk road north of Wormhout. Here they were joined by Captain Sir John Nicholson (4th Cheshires), who had also escaped from Wormhout with a small party of his men. The combined group reached Wylder without incident, and were glad to meet the CO and his party.

After a conference with the Brigadier, the CO was ordered to proceed with his men to Rexpoede, which was crammed with British and French troops. Three lines of transport en route for Dunkirk had absolutely jammed the main road of the small town.

Those who had escaped had fought bravely, and without yielding their positions until surrender was the only alternative. But in Wormhout, men remained to whom a way out was impossible – the prisoners, some of whom were to undergo an almost unspeakable ordeal, and the wounded, many of whom were to survive solely because of the unflagging attentions of the Medical Officer and his handful of helpers.

There were also some men, mainly of 'B' Company, who were the isolated and scattered remnants of a brave fighting force.

'I was very worried', said Bill Cordrey, as he continued his narrative, 'because Clancy had been away for more than half-an-hour. Also, things were very quiet, and although I welcomed the respite, its significance was alarming.

'Suddenly, I heard a voice behind me and Clancy jumped into the trench. One look at his face was sufficient for me. We were in trouble. I waited for him to recover his breath, and then he made his report.

'He had made his way to Company HQ. There must have been

one hell of a scrap there. Trucks smashed. Houses burning. Dead bodies everywhere. He said that he nearly went into Wormhout, but decided not to because he had been told to get back as soon as possible. On the way he met Platoon Sergeant-Major Agutter who was in a dazed condition, which Clancy thought was due to shell-shock.

'I went to where Agutter had been left, and realized that he was in need of medical attention. There was only one thing for it, and that was to make for Wormhout and get him to the Medical Officer.

'As the lads mounted the bren back in the carrier, Clancy and I got the Sergeant-Major on board and having made sure that the gun was ready for firing, the order was given to move off. Even before we got into the town I could see that it was hopeless, for the whole place was burning and I decided to make for Dunkirk. So we went tearing down the road, flat out. It was Dunkirk, or bust . . .

'Suddenly, I remembered the road-block. Could we break through it? If it hadn't been reinforced, we could.

'Every second brought us nearer, and Clancy looked at me. "Keep going and we'll break through", I yelled. In fact, we were now on top of it and I could see that it had been reinforced.

'I screamed at Clancy: "Slow down and spin round!"'

'At the same time, all hell was let loose. We were being absolutely plastered with machine-gun fire. I sprayed the road-block with the bren, in reply.

'Now, a good driver can spin a carrier round on a sixpence. And Clancy was a good driver. We started to turn – and then, out of the corner of my eye, I could see an anti-tank gun being brought to bear on us. It was on the other side of the road. "O God", I thought, "this is it, they can't miss".

'It must have taken a couple of seconds for the carrier to turn, but it seemed like hours. I could see the barrel of the gun being brought down on us. It was all happening in slow motion. I remember saying, "turn, you b . . . .".

'And then, we were off!

'As we moved forward, I saw a red flash from the gun. But we kept going. They had fired, and missed! We were now speeding back towards Wormhout.

' "Everybody OK?" I yelled.

' "I think the Sergeant-Major has had it", said Ginger.

'Taking a quick look, I saw that he was beyond our help. The four of us were still OK, but how long would our luck hold out? We were approaching Wormhout again, and from this angle it looked as though everything was burning.

"When we were nearly up to the Church, Clancy broke into my thoughts. "Which way, Corporal?", he shouted.

'I took a bet, and said: "Left".

'He spun the wheel hard round, and within seconds we were half out of the town. I began to think that it was surely time we dumped the carrier when to my horror I saw that we were going to pass hundreds of Germans!

'Suddenly, the carrier spun out of control. We had hit a shell-hole in the road. Desperately, Clancy tried to recover, but it was too late. Veering across the road, we finished up nose first in a ditch.

'Immediately, we were surrounded by German troops.. The situation was hopeless and I told the lads to put up their hands. One look at the Jerries was enough to convince me that a false move on our part would start them shooting.

'We were told to get out of the carrier by a German who spoke a little English. I got out, and as soon as I had put my feet on the ground, another German came running up. Sticking a big revolver in my stomach, he started screaming at me in German.

'I could feel the tension building up around us. There seemed to be hundreds of them surrounding us but this one was blowing his top! Looking down at the revolver, I saw that his hand was shaking.

' "Any second now", I thought, "and he's going to pull the trigger."

'Suddenly, he turned away from me and shouted an order to the others – and about thirty of them doubled off down the road in the direction we had come from. I then realised that he was trying to find out if there were any more of us.

'He seemed to be a senior NCO, and was certainly looking

trigger-happy, so I was very relieved when, after shouting a few more orders, he put his revolver away and made off down the road.

'During this time, it had begun to rain.

'We were then marched over to a large, open-sided barn, and the one who spoke English gave us a cigarette. I looked at our captors and couldn't help feeling impressed by their general turn-out. They all seemed young and intelligent, and very much alert. In contrast, we must have looked a scruffy bunch.

'As we were being marched away, I took a look at our old carrier. She was absolutely pickled with holes! How we had got away from the road-block, I shall never know. From the gesticulations of the Germans, I could see that our vehicle was the cause of much discussion.

'I asked them if we could bury Platoon Sergeant-Major Agutter, but they said that it would be attended to. They added that all information concerning us would be sent to the Red Cross.'

CHAPTER EIGHT

The Massacre

Around the time Bill Cordrey was taken prisoner, Reginald West was being escorted across a large field. He supposed that he was being taken to the farmhouse which was immediately ahead, but as they drew nearer, the Germans appeared to have another destination in mind. West was intrigued because, although there was another house in the distance, they seemed to be making for a clump of trees. Then he saw that their objective was the meadow adjacent to the trees and on entering it, he saw a column of men, most of whom he recognised. The men at the head of the column were already going into a barn situated near a row of trees which enclosed one side of the meadow and when he was joined to the column, it seemed reasonable to suppose that the barn was being used as a makeshift depot for the temporary reception of prisoners.

The fact that it had just begun to shower with rain led John Lavelle to conclude that they were going inside to keep dry. Richard Parry imputed the same charitable motive to the SS-guards.

But although the shower dried up almost as soon as it had started, the men were still ordered inside the building, which was guarded by twelve Germans. Eight covered the open gable-end entrance, which had no doors. Another four faced the length of the barn, which had a small doorway at the opposite end to the main entrance. [1]

[1] The four Germans who covered the length of the building were from the *Leibstandarte*'s 2nd Battalion, Seven Company, and had themselves taken some of the prisoners. The others were a special escort from the Signals section of Eight Company, selected specifically for this task.

As the men made their way into the barn – to the accompaniment of loud shouts, in German – it occurred to those outside that there would be insufficient room for all of them. So Richard Parry (whose efforts to help his wounded comrade led to his being at the end of the file) elbowed his way through, to join an Artillery pal who had gone in to the back of the building.

Meanwhile none of the guards or prisoners knew that they were being watched by a man who lay hidden behind the nearby hedge.

The astonished spectator was Private George Merry, of 'D' Company, who had been wounded in the arm during the German attack. On hearing the command 'Every man for himself!', he was alarmed to find that he was being left where he had fallen. Near at hand was the body of Private Wheatley, who was killed by the burst which wounded Merry.

Shortly after the others had scattered, he was terrified to see a number of Germans approaching him. Helpless, he could only lie as still as the nearby corpse, close his eyes, and hope. Miraculously, they seemed not to notice him; and when they had gone, he staggered to his feet and dragged himself along. When he reached the edge of the meadow, he was in a state of collapse and, watching the prisoners going into the barn, he wondered if he was hallucinated as the result of his condition. Stupefied, he guessed what was about to happen, and shivered lest he should be discovered and joined to the waiting occupants of the barn.

The fates of War had staged an awful drama for him to witness. As his eyes moistened, he bit his lips.

When Bert Evans reached the doorway he saw that there was no room inside and a few men, of whom he was one, were crowded in the entrance. Next to him was his Company Commander, Captain Lynn-Allen, the only officer in the party. Evans respected him for staying close to his men when the fighting was at its bloodiest, especially after hearing some men complain that they had not seen an officer during the whole day's fighting.

Lynn-Allen was not intimidated by the brutality of the SS-guards, and stated that he was going to protest about the way some of the men were being treated.

When a German approached, he said: 'I wish to complain that there are wounded men inside, and there is not enough room for them to lie down.'

Looking sarcastic, the guard answered cryptically in English, with an American accent: 'Yellow Englishman, there will be plenty of room where you are going.'

Evans thought he was referring to the generous proportions of the camp for which they were destined, but Lynn-Allen shook his head and said, 'I am not satisfied.'

The look on the German's face changed to one of malevolence, and he reddened with anger. In the same instant, he reached down for the stick-grenade which protruded from his boot, and with an over-arm motion, lobbed it amongst the prisoners.

The noise of the explosion was so deafening that Evans felt an intense pressure in his ears. He was also conscious of a numb feeling in his right arm. Looking down, he saw blood pouring down the shattered limb. Strangely, he felt no pain.

But he was given no time for further consideration of his condition, because as the fragments from the grenade flew in all directions, the Germans ran for cover – and Lynn-Allen seized the opportunity to drag Evans clear.

Pulling the wounded man by the left arm, he shouted, 'Quick! Run for it,' and as they sprinted from the doorway they heard two shots. Together, they ran along the tree-lined edge of the meadow, making for the clump of trees at the end: and for a distance of about two hundred yards, the Captain supported Evans.

As they made their way, Lynn-Allen urged, 'Keep going, and stay low!'

Breathless, they reached the clump of trees, some of which were on the edge of a small pond of stagnant water. Lynn-Allen took a quick look, and without hesitation pulled his companion after him into the pond. With the water reaching up to their chests, they were partly hidden.

'Get down!' Lynn-Allen ordered, 'and keep your arm out of the water.'

Crouching low, they heard sounds which told them that someone was running in their direction: and suddenly, a German appeared.

Armed with a revolver, he pointed it at Lynn-Allen from close range and fired, twice.

The Captain cried, 'Oh! my God', and slumped into the water. Evans had seen the bullet pierce his forehead, and knew that he was dead . . .

The German then fired two shots at Evans, who was standing near a tree situated on the water's edge. The bullets hit the tree-trunk, ricocheted, and hit him in the neck. As Evans fell forward in the pond, the German grunted and moved off, undoubtedly satisfied that each man had been disposed of: and Evans groped in the bottom of the pond, but failed to find the officer's body. Desperately, he wanted to run from the scene, but by this time had come to value the exercise of caution and so, inclining his head, he listened carefully.

From the direction of the barn came the sounds of shots and screams; and as the teenaged soldier considered the plight of his comrades, his inability to help them overcame him, and he wept.

When he scrambled out of the pond he was momentarily constrained to go back, but prudence pulled him in the other direction and carefully he walked through the trees, feeling very sad. Looking ahead, he saw a farmhouse which was well within his capacity to reach – but as he staggered in its direction he felt a sudden, searing pain across the top of his shoulders. In the same instant, he heard the crack of a rifle. Collapsing to the ground he guessed that the marksman was about a hundred yards away, and lay still until he was satisfied that he was not being pursued.

Regaining his feet he recommenced his journey with faltering steps, and eventually reeled into the farmyard – and there, not many yards away from him, a German soldier was bending over a motor-cycle combination . . .

On hearing the injured man's approach the German walked towards him. Imagining the worst, Bert said, 'Please get it over with, and don't mess around'; but to his surprise, the German placed him gently on the ground and motioned for him to lie still. He then walked over to a clothes-line, pulled down a sheet, and tore it into strips. Moving back, he bound up Bert's arm, placed him carefully in the sidecar and covered him with a German greatcoat.

When Bert was being driven away, he wondered where they were going, but eventually they reached a field dressing station and it was shortly after the machine had come to a halt that there was a hint of more trouble.

With much commotion, a German officer rushed towards the man who had befriended Evans and began to remonstrate with him. Then he moved over and pulled the greatcoat away – but when he caught sight of the shattered arm his attitude changed, and he apologised to the two men.

On examining the arm, a doctor said that it would have to be amputated, with the operation taking place in hospital; and after receiving first-aid, the wounded man was taken to Boulogne. During the operation the hospital was hit by the British, who were shelling Boulogne, but Evans was unharmed.

That he lived to tell his amazing story was due to the exceptional bravery of Captain Lynn-Allen, who had proved himself a worthy officer and courageous gentleman. Also, Evans had met some Germans whose chivalry and kindness had preserved his life.

After the grenade which injured Evans had exploded, the noise from the prisoners was loud and intense. Those who were hidden from the doorway shouted their queries and protests. A few men at the back, imagining that one of their number had attacked the Germans, raised a cheer. The wounded screamed. Above the pandemonium, Company Sergeant-Major Jennings and Sergeant Moore called loudly for order; and with the exception of the wounded, who could not forbear to groan, the men became silent.

Suddenly, another grenade was thrown in the direction of the two NCOs who, in a calculated act of bravery and without thought for their own safety, stifled it with their bodies so as to shield others from the effects of the explosion.

The two men died, instantly.

Again and again, more grenades were thrown at irregular intervals and the little building was filled with the screams and groans of those who suffered the impact of shrapnel, which buried itself into their flesh. Many men were already dead.

Richard Parry counted five explosions, each of which caused him to tremble. One actually blew him partly through the side of the barn, leaving only his legs inside. One of his legs had been wounded, and he was unable to move. However, with the top half of his body protruding through the wall of the barn, he was placed in a situation which enabled him to see much of that which followed outside.

Private John Lavelle was in pain from a shrapnel wound in his foot, and leaning against the wall, peered through a crack. This enabled him to witness one of the acts of barbarism which followed on his side of the barn.

When the last grenade had been thrown, the Germans yelled out words of command: and although he could not speak German, Lavelle was able to make out that '*Raus!*' had something to do with going outside. A neighbour translated the command.

'They're demanding that five men should go outside', he said.

There was a natural reluctance on the part of the prisoners to obey the command which, within a few seconds, was barked out again. Then, Alf Tombs heard a man say, 'Come on, if we've got to go, we've got to go . . . '

He was the first to emerge, and four others followed. The men walked slowly, with heads held high; and the little procession was led to a point on the right-hand side of the doorway, and about twenty yards away.

An armed guard stood facing each prisoner, thus forming a rough firing-squad: and the awful intention of the Germans became quite clear to the helpless men who faced them. One man asked if they could smoke: 'Just one, last cigarette,' but this mercy was refused; and those who were watching through the cracks in the walls, began to express their disgust.

The five men were ordered to turn around.

Their comrades inside the barn became quiet, and even the wounded ceased to moan. Some who were peering through the cracks, averted their eyes. The shots rang out with a dull, short stutter and the five men fell to the ground.

As he watched, John Lavelle noticed that one of the men was still alive and felt sure that he was feigning death.

The executioners had by no means finished, for without glancing at the bodies lying on the grass, they strode back to the entrance and yelled for five more men to come out.

Emerging slowly, the men who had elected to meet their executioners were taken to a spot on the left-hand side of the barn . . .

Richard Parry was lying with the top half of his body outside the barn and, being placed in a corner, was able to witness the shooting of each group. He saw that again, the men were ordered to turn around: but as the guards prepared to fire at the back of their heads, the men swivelled on their heels and faced the brutes who, seconds later, became their murderers.

Immediately, pandemonium broke out in the barn as many of those inside began to voice their loud protests, but the executioners hurried back to the doorway. Pointing their rifles, they roughly demanded that five more men should come out.

This time, there was a stubborn refusal from the herded captives, and the guards began to confer with each other. As they talked, there was a sudden and torrential downpour of rain. [2]This hastened the resolve of the Germans, who had no desire to become drenched as they dealt out death – and instantly, they stormed into the barn.

The men near the entrance were ordered to turn around, and were shot in the back. One of these was Charles Daley, who already had been wounded in the shoulder at the time of his capture.

Moving further into the barn, the Germans trampled on the dead and the wounded as they opened fire with their automatic weapons, spraying bullets in all directions.

The barn was filled with smoke. Many of the dead lay on top of each other, and several men crawled under the bodies for protection. So many had rushed towards the sides of the building that bodies were piled up against the walls. Due to the crowded conditions, the wounded were half-standing, or collapsed in most awkward positions.

[2] There are two references in the Battalion Diary which make mention of the weather. An item for 1445 hours says: 'At this time a violent thunderstorm was raging, and the rain was pouring down.' This fell at the time of Tombs' capture. Later, there is a phrase: 'Troops being soaked to the skin', timed at 1700 hours. This would be the time of the massacre. Apart from these heavy outbreaks, there were occasional showers (as when the men were filing into the barn).

Some men died with photographs of their families in their hands . . .

As the shooting continued, Charles Daley was hit again (this time, in the leg) and became unconscious. Richard Parry (whose trunk and shoulders were still in the open air) received another bullet, in the foot. He blacked out with pain. Alf Tombs had been badly wounded in the shin, but felt no pain. Indeed, he was unaware of having received a wound. As he lay on the ground, he heard a man cry out: 'Shoot me, shoot me!' There was a single shot, and the short groan which was added to the other cries indicated that the plea had been answered . . .

A corporal, the bottom part of whose face had been blown away, died as he was being comforted by his neighbour, who shouted, 'What a bloody way to die!'

Lying in a pile of cow manure, Private George Hopper hardly noticed the weight of the bodies which lay on top of him. Within inches of his head was a face whose frozen features stared at him . . .

One fair-haired young soldier lay close to George Hall in a terribly mutilated condition. Slowly, he began to stammer the Lord's Prayer. Each syllable was slower than the last, and when he completed the petition, 'Hallowed by Thy Name', he exhaled heavily, and died.

George Hall finished the prayer, with several others joining in.

Glancing around, he felt physically sick as he caught sight of a man writhing on the floor whose thigh had been peppered with bullets, and was twisted in the leg of his trousers. He was beating the ground with such frenzied agony that George thought, 'He'll surely go mad.'

Then he realized that the shooting had stopped, and decided that, whatever the outcome, he was going to attempt a break-out. But a movement in the doorway told him that the entrance was still guarded, so he crawled quickly to the back of the building. Peering through a crack in the wall, he saw no Germans on that side of the barn. Looking down, he saw that a bottom plank looked quite rotten and after pulling hard, managed to dislodge it. As he prepared to crawl though the aperture, a voice cried out, 'For God's sake, don't go – it's not safe.'

'I've had enough of waiting here, to be killed,' he replied, as he wriggled into the open air.

Crawling frantically, he reached the hedge, scratching his face and arms badly as he made his way through, but was so intent on escape that he felt no pain. From his position on the other side of the hedge, he heard the cries of the men. Also there were German voices and shots. For the moment he felt safe, and resolved to stay put until the Germans had gone.

As they were preparing to go, one of the guards noticed Richard Parry's body protruding from the barn wall and walked over to him. At the same time, Parry recovered consciousness and found that he was looking up at a figure which was silhouetted against the sky. Shading his eyes with his hand, he saw the German standing over him . . . with a rifle pointed at his head.

On catching sight of the German, Parry was moved to call him by some uncomplimentary English names. At the same time, he placed one hand on the ground and lifted himself up, so as to look the Nazi full in the face.

When the weapon was fired, Parry's mouth was wide open – and the bullet entered between his teeth, coming out at the back of the jaw. He became unconscious.

It was the last bullet of the massacre; and with their task accomplished, the SS-guards left the meadow under the watchful eye of George Merry, who became increasingly horrified as the Germans approached the hedge behind which he was hiding.

As the Germans drew nearer, he felt himself becoming quite cold. Shivering, he realized that his only chance of survival was to lie still, so as (for the second time in that day) to convey the impression that he was dead.

With his eyes closed, he whispered, 'God help me'.

In the same moment, he felt a sharp prod and opened his eyes. Standing over him was the guard who had been the last to leave the meadow. The muzzle of his weapon was touching George's face, and he knew that he was about to be shot. However, instead of firing his rifle, the German rapped out a word of command and motioned for George to put his hands above his head – but when he tried to comply, the injured arm would not move. The German

Charles Daley, 'A' Company

Alfred Tombs, 'HQ' Company

Wormhout Square looking south

26 rue d'eglise where the prisoners were held before being taken to the barn

Albert Evans, D' Company   George Hall, 'D' Company, Signals

The pool where Captain Lynn-Allen was killed (in front of the tree on the left). Private Evans also hid in this pool.

bent down and examined the arm. Straightening up, he gave George a push with his boot which caused him to roll over. This done, the German grunted and walked on. George could hardly believe his luck as he watched the guards making their way back to their Battalion HQ.

Officially, they had 'disposed of' about 90 men: but in reality, they had participated in a most fiendish and heinous massacre. All mass-murder is revolting, but the killings in the meadow at Esquelbecq were unspeakably inhuman on account of their protracted nature.

There was the maltreatment of the 'stragglers' on the fateful march to the meadow. The tossing in of the grenades. The ordering out of the captives in groups of five – such a clumsy operation that not all the men were executed. The cowardly shooting of the men inside the barn – and again, so botched-up that at least one man was left to agonise. The spraying of the remaining prisoners with automatic weapons – likewise bungled, as the moans and screams of the wounded and dying so pathetically testified.

It becomes difficult to believe that the armed dunces who perpetrated such an outrage were professional soldiers of an élite Regiment; for many hours later, several men in the meadow remained convulsed in misery and anguish.

On arrival at Battalion HQ, the SS-guards heard that 'Sepp' Dietrich had been rescued at 1700 hours from the ditch where he had been in hiding for the greater part of the day, and being uninjured had returned to Regimental HQ at Esquelbecq.

His absence had caused great inconvenience for, apart from the psychological effect of the loss of their Commander, the *Leibstandarte* was prevented from using its artillery in attempts to dislodge the British from the Esquelbecq-Wormhout road area. Reconnaissance parties had established that Dietrich's car had been damaged on the bend of the road, and it was hopefully presumed that 'Sepp' had taken cover in the vicinity of the car. Shelling of the area would endanger his life.

In the early afternoon, a party of hand-picked men from Six Company was sent out to establish Dietrich's position, and rescue him. In their determined efforts, they set fire to a farmhouse which was being used by a platoon of the Cheshires, but were repulsed. Successive attempts were checked, and Sturmbannführer Trabandt (who had taken over in Dietrich's absence) was furious when informed of the failure of the operation.

When Dietrich was returned to Regimental HQ by a unit of the Army, his staff, though pleased to see Dietrich, were enraged that the Army had succeeded where the SS had failed, and tempers became frayed . . .

It was at this time that Hauptsturmführer Alfred Ebner arrived at Dietrich's Headquarters, to report on posting to the *Leibstandarte*.

Ebner had come to Wormhout from the Marine Commando station, 'Baltic', to obtain battle experience. The order for his attachment was made by Himmler, as the promising young officer's career was being carefully supervised.

The Chief Officer of the Waffen-SS in Berlin ordered him to depart immediately for the last known position of the *Leibstandarte*, and arriving at St Omer on 27th May, he was told that the Regiment had crossed the canal at Watten. Proceeding to Divisional HQ, he was informed that he had missed meeting Dietrich, who had gone into the British lines and was presumed to have been captured. Later, the Divisional Commander told him that Dietrich had been rescued by men of the Armoured Division, but only after SS-troops had failed to recover him.

Arriving at the *Leibstandarte*'s Regimental HQ, Ebner was strictly informed that the claims of the Army to have captured Dietrich were grossly exaggerated, as the SS had liberated their Commander themselves! Also, he was ordered not to repeat what he had been told – especially to Dietrich, as the incident had created a bad atmosphere. On meeting Dietrich, he was warned by the Obergruppenführer to be careful, and Ebner realized that he knew too much about the affair.

He was ordered to take over from the platoon leader who had temporarily replaced Mohnke as Commander of Five Company

CHAPTER NINE

Beaches for Some

George Hopper was one of the few men who were physically unharmed and amongst the first to leave the barn when the Germans left, but unfortunately recaptured within a very short time. With the intention of finding help for the wounded, he made his cautious way along the hedgerows. It was not long before he reached a farmhouse and after some hesitation decided to go inside, only to step into a room which was filled with Germans.

Hardly more fortunate was the experience of Alf Tombs who found it almost impossible to believe that the nightmarish cruelties had come to an end, but heard someone say that one or two men had got away.

For the first time since entering the barn, he was able to give some rational thought to the situation. First, he noticed that his back was covered with blood from the two bodies which had lain on top of him. Then, he looked around and saw that corpses were piled up along the walls. There were wounded men whose pain was desperate, particularly the soldier whose leg had been shattered, and who was 'punching the ground in agony'. Equally grim was the sight of Sergeant Moore's body, for Alf and the Sergeant had been old chums. Their wives were also friendly, and there had been cordial links with the Sergeant's mother . . .

He and the other men in his part of the barn did their utmost to help the wounded, but lacked medical supplies and realised the need of skilled assistance which they agreed should be sought forthwith. After some argument as to whether or not they should go together, it was decided that it would be unwise to split up.

With difficulty they emerged from the barn, for the main

entrance was crammed with bodies, so the five men left through the small doorway. In addition to Tombs, they were: Corporal Gill, Privates Dutton and Cooper, and Lance-Corporal Box.

As they crawled along the ditch, which was so waterlogged as to resemble a moat, they were too anxious to notice their discomfort. Eventually it was necessary for them to cross an open field but on reaching the shelter of the corner hedge they were mortified to see a small group of Germans emerging through a gap. Smartly, they closed in, with weapons at the ready.

Suddenly, one of the escapers decided that freedom was worth the risk of making a dash for it, but as he sprinted for the hedge, a German promptly fired at him. From the look of satisfaction on the German's face, Tombs had no doubt that his friend had been killed.

The following incident was equally surprising to Germans and prisoners when, as the marksman turned back, one of the remaining captives fell down on his knees; and looking up at the German, implored, as he sobbed, 'Don't shoot me, please don't shoot me, my mother's only got one son now.' He was in his late teens, and Tombs knew that he was referring to the fact that his brother had died in the barn.

If natural, his fears were unfounded, for the Germans seemed amiably disposed towards the prisoners: and as Tombs and the others recognised, it had been legitimate for the SS-guard to prevent the prisoner's escape. However, the German motioned to the kneeling soldier that there was no need for anxiety, and he stood up, still trembling.

Then, a German officer who was possessed of a pleasant manner and spoke perfect English, approached. He said, 'It's all right, boys. For you the war is over. We will soon be in London and you will be sent to work in Berlin.'

Afterwards, the four men were taken to the main road and handed over to a German Army unit. As there was some confusion as to where the prisoners were going, they were allowed to sit down on the side of the road for about an hour.

Passing Germans cheerfully threw biscuits, which turned out to be plundered British rations! They also seemed to have been successful in a raid on a cellar, for as they walked past some were holding bottles to their mouths. Tombs and the others were even offered some of the wine to drink, but although they were parched with thirst, they considered it wise to refuse.

Before joining the Army, Reginald West had worked as a miner and was accustomed to labouring for long stretches in confined conditions. He had seen gruesome accidents at the coal face and had assisted in bringing out men whose limbs had been mangled, yet he was feeling quite claustrophobic from the effects of the conditions in the barn. He was also affected by the sight of so many bodies with limbs which had been shattered into inhuman and grotesque positions.

His first-aid experience was too limited to enable him to be of any assistance to the man who was crying so pathetically for his mother, so he decided to try and get through to Battalion HQ in an attempt to obtain medical treatment for the wounded.

Emerging from the barn he crawled carefully along the ditch, for he could hear sounds of enemy activity in the immediate vicinity. He appreciated the necessity of finding a way which afforded adequate cover. His underground experience had accustomed him to long periods on his hands and knees, so he was not tempted to take that one short cut in the open which would be disastrous.

It proved to be a long and uncomfortable journey which presented several hazards, but his carefulness was rewarded when he reached the spinney which was near his objective. Though weary, he remained alert and trod carefully so as to avoid cracking any twigs and fallen branches.

Then he heard a faint moaning which came from the direction of a nearby bush. Moving with great care he was surprised to see Major Harborne, lying near to Private White. Each man had been wounded, and the officer seemed to be in a serious condition. Bending over the wounded men were Sergeant Plant and Private Herbert, who greeted West enthusiastically and told him that they had been wondering how to remove the two wounded men – for the place was alive with Germans, with the occasional shot coming as a reminder that resistance was still being offered.

Suddenly, a voice said, 'You'd better come out!'

It was RSM Turner.

The Sergeant-Major quickly assumed control of the situation, and the officer was carried out on an overcoat. White was helped to hobble along.

Prior to the arrival of the Sergeant-Major, West had gathered that the HQ position had been over-run, with the CO and others having escaped. In the circumstances, help for the men in the barn was hopeless. Quickly, he thought the matter out. If the Germans were in occupation of the sector and it was 'every man for himself', he was adamant that, having been in the hands of the Germans once, he was not going to fall foul of them again. Alone, he could use his own initiative.

He refused to come out! In normal circumstances such disobedience would have been most imprudent, for a Regimental Sergeant-Major was an object of compulsory respect – but the circumstances of the moment were such that rank mattered little, and respect was a quality in its own right. In any case, he had seen such horrible things taking place at the hands of the SS, that a Sergeant-Major's bark was of little consequence.

However, the RSM had other things on his mind than the stubbornness of human nature and was only concerned with getting the wounded men out.

Alone in his hiding place, West could hear the occasional shot and wondered how long it would be before the last round was fired. He was surprised that any of the defenders were still fighting. Although it had been a hot day with heavy thunderstorms, it was becoming cold with the fading light and he decided that it was opportune to move out. If he stayed in the bushes all night, his chances of being undiscovered in the morning were slim. So he moved out, not knowing which way to take, and yet confident that his intuition would serve him to pick the right way. After a few minutes he saw the gloomy outlines of houses, and felt sure that they were unoccupied and that he would be right to make them his objective.

Wearily, he moved along. Here and there were signs of the day's fighting. The ground was littered with the discarded tools of war, and the occasional body. The mud had been churned up by a variety of vehicles. From one or two of the houses, an occasional flame curled into the sky.

As he drew level with the houses, he thought, 'Now for it. I'll look well if the one I choose is being used by Jerry.' So he decided to make for the house which was sufficiently damaged as to inhibit anyone from using it. Inside, the room was amazingly tidy and although the windows were broken and part of the wall shattered, the furniture was just as it had been left.

It seemed safe, so he went upstairs to ensure that the house was unoccupied. But when he saw the bed, he realized how weary he was. Taking off his boots, he lay down and marvelled that it could be so quiet. Despite his intention to remain alert, he fell asleep.

George Hall was similarly successful in evading the Germans, but his resting place for the night was less comfortable as he lay down under the stars, shivering with cold. Unaware of his situation, all he knew was that he was on the outskirts of Wormhout.

Also ignorant of the place where they were resting for the night was a party of prisoners which included Captain Tomes, whose account provides details of his capture and subsequent treatment. This was supplemented by Private Albert Montague, of 'A' Company, in a statement made after the war and which was useful in establishing that prisoners who were captured after 1700 hours received normal POW treatment. Montague was a stretcher bearer, and had brought in two wounded men to the First Aid Post, which was in the cellar of a house. The Medical Officer and his orderly, Lance-Corporal Lodge, were busy, and Montague was asked to stay and give such assistance as was required.

By this time, Captain Tomes had been brought in by a couple of stretcher bearers. Also, those men who needed hospital treatment kept the ambulance driver busy, and during the morning and early afternoon, he had made several journeys. Montague had been helping the Medical Officer for about four hours when the driver returned to report that whichever way he went, his vehicle had suffered attack.

After making his report he returned to his vehicle, but ran back almost immediately with the news that it had been hit and was on fire.

At about the same time, news was received that several wounded men were in the house next door, and as the MO went out with some stretcher-bearers, he was confronted by a couple of young SS-soldiers who were armed with automatic rifles. One of them repeated the legend which would appear to have been compulsory learning in the *Leibstandarte*: 'Tommy, the war is over for you'. In reply, Captain Crooks told the Germans that he was in charge of a First Aid Post and that his duty was to stay with the wounded, but permission was refused. Despite the protests of the Medical Officer, the seriously wounded were left behind and the party, which included the walking-wounded, was marched for about twenty minutes. On the way, Captain Tomes noticed the body of Captain Padfield, lying at the corner of a field.

When the party reached the new German HQ (Le Fort Rose Farm), they noticed a barn which was near a brick wall. Lined up against the barn, were about 25 prisoners who were faced by two armed SS-guards. As the new arrivals were joined to the waiting party, they noticed the machine-gun which had been set up.

The men were searched and allowed to retain their pay-books. All other belongings, including wrist-watches and rings, were thrown to the ground. Montague had some family photographs in his possession, but these were torn to pieces by the German who was making the search.

The prisoners were kept at the farm for about three hours, and during the whole of this time were compelled to stand with their hands behind their backs, and forbidden to talk. When Captain Crooks pleaded for permission to return to the wounded there was some argument, but the Germans gave permission for him to return to the First Aid Post under an armed escort of ten men, led by Hauptsturmführer Drescher. The MO led the Germans to the cellar, where about 25 men were treated; and the whole contingent then returned to the German lines, where Crooks was allowed to make his patients comfortable.

The German version of what followed was given by SS-Schütze Hans Koriaka, who stated that the MO asked 'if he could go to a place where a certain Major was lying', but as it was too far away, the Germans refused to go – and Crook was allowed to make his way alone!

The German said, 'I never saw the British Captain again.'

Tomes records a different, and more likely version: ' . .the Doctor escaped from the guard, collected several wounded (including Harborne), put them into a lorry and drove off under the very eyes of the Germans: but after driving all night and part of the next day trying to get to Dunkirk, was re-captured.'

Tomes, Montague and the other prisoners were taken at 2130 hours by lorry to a schoolroom which was a few miles from Wormhout and whose location was a mystery. The building was already crowded with prisoners, and it was impossible for many to lie down. The tired men spent a most uncomfortable night.

Meanwhile, the Commanding Officer and the remnants of his Battalion were billeted in empty houses of Rexpoede for the night. Some of the men were fortunate to discover clean civilian clothes, into which they changed.

The men settled down to sleep, and the diary reads: 'Darkness came down, but lines of transport continued on their way all night . . . '

But the meagre handful of men who remained in Wormhout stubbornly refused to abandon their task – as Fritz Bütler, adjutant of the *Leibstandarte*'s 2nd Battalion, testified: 'Sometime before midnight, wild shooting broke out near Battalion HQ. Sentries from the covering positions rushed in, and reported: "The British are here!" All available runners and drivers were sent out in the darkness to the danger point and in a few minutes, all was quiet again . . . The companies were ordered to muster for the coming night and to draw up, platoon by platoon on the northerly and north-easterly edge, as though defending a strong-point.'

Referring to what must have been the same incident, the diarist of 'B' Company recorded:

Recce. towards centre with CSM, to find out what was happening. Sounded as though right platoon engaging Germans down through Railway embankment. Boche coming in. Retreated.

Otto Baum stated: 'I was ordered by Mohnke to withdraw those
parts which had penetrated into the village, as he expected heavy
enemy fire on Wormhout during the night. I was to continue to
block the road coming from the south and to look for contact on the
right. The further order was that the Battalion was to push through
Wormhout at daybreak and to attack in a general north-easterly
direction. When it was dark and rations had been issued, I drove to
Six Company, to confer with the Commander, Obersturmführer
Anhalt about the deployment of the attack during the next day. As
it was completely dark, we studied our maps by the light of the still
burning houses. I went to bed, because I was very tired.'

At 2300 hours, the weary Dietrich looked back on a singularly
eventful birthday and penned his final comment that the battle was
over . . .

Other German commanders in the area were equally weary, for
at Wylder, two companies of the 8th Worcesters had resisted with
vigour, and a troop of the Worcestershire Yeomanry (under Major
R. Wiggin) destroyed 24 German tanks. The gallant 5th
Gloucesters in nearby Ledringhem were reduced to 200 men, who
fought their way out at the point of the bayonet: and the 143 survivors, with wounded in wheelbarrows and on a couple of
carthorses, made their way through the German lines after dark –
capturing three of the enemy as they escaped.

On 29th May, reveille for the men in Rexpoede was at 0530
hours, and as the town was considered to be vulnerable to attack
from the air they were moved out to the east, on the road to Killem.
Breakfast, though consisting of bully beef and biscuits, was most
welcome – as was the new clothing which was issued to all ranks
from the Quartermaster's lorry.

Seven more men, including Captain E. Jerram, arrived from
Wormhout, having walked through the night.

At 0900 hours, all vehicles with the exception of the water-cart
were put out of action, after having been driven on to a field. An
hour later, the men were moved a distance of about two miles to the
situation of Brigade HQ, and the Battalion was re-organised after

Major P. H. W. Hicks had been informed by the Brigadier that he had been promoted to lieutenant-colonel.

The appointments were:

Commanding Officer: Lieutenant-Colonel P. H. W. Hicks, MC
Second in Command: Captain E. Jerram
Adjutant: 2nd Lieutenant J. W. Tomes
Quartermaster: Lieutenant S. Williams
RSM: PSM Chambers
1 Platoon – 2nd Lieutenant J. Vaudrey   (37 men)
2 Platoon – PSM Dixon   (18 men)
3 Platoon – Sergeant Bell   (18 men)
4 Platoon – 2nd Lieutenant Wright   (19 men)
5 Platoon – Sergeant A. Brown, MM   (18 men)
6 Platoon – 2nd Lieutenant Davis   (20 men)

Arthur Johnson states that shared out between the platoons, were 4 Brens and 2 anti-tank rifles, with ammunition for about five minutes firing.

From 1100 hours until midnight was a most frustrating period, with orders received and cancelled. In the early afternoon, an interesting diversion was provided when two men arrived, one carrying a bren and the other, a box of ammunition. Introducing themselves as members of the Highland Light Infantry, they asked if they could attach themselves to the Battalion.

Sergeant Humphries had a portable radio which was switched on for the nine o'clock news from London, during which it was announced that after the news, a Major who had escaped from Dunkirk would give an account of his experiences. The announcement was received by all with loud cat-calls!

The rest of the story from the war diary, reads:

2000 hours. Orders cancelled. Position to be held until 2400 hours. Some firing heard in distance. Continual shelling by own guns in direction of Wylder. Some white Very lights seen presumably enemy. 2400 hours. Movement started for Bray Dunes. Brigade staff and attached personnel leading all on foot followed by the 6 platoons. Route: X-roads 3576 – road & canal Br. 3578 – road junc. 3582 – road junc. 3384 – Chyvelde – road & canal br. 3588 – Bray Dunes, the long looked-for beach. On march passed thousands of lorries and guns lining the roadside, all abandoned and put out of action. In some cases, so close were they together that it was with difficulty that anybody was able to pass by. Some were smouldering having been set alight, it is thought, by 5th Columnists, because they lit up the countryside, and on a clear night made the marching personnel an excellent target from the air.

The beach at Bray Dunes was reached at 0500 hours on 30th May, and the first men left at 1000 hours. The last man to get away, left at 2350 hours.

Arthur Johnson recalls that when the depleted Battalion arrived on the crowded sands, Major Hicks formed the men up into three ranks and marched them forward, shouting, 'Make way for the 2nd Battalion of the Royal Warwickshire Regiment!'

Remarkably, a gap was created for the CO and his men to march through.

At the water's edge, a boat was seen floating some distance away. Hicks shouted, 'Get it!' Johnson obeyed and found that there was a large hole in the hull. The hole was stuffed with an overcoat and the little craft was towed out to a coastal vessel by a boat with a naval rating aboard. Crowded with troops, the ship landed in Ramsgate.

One indiscreetly bumptious officer was nearly tipped out of a small boat in mid-Channel, according to a soldier who remembered being sent from Brigade HQ to Wormhout for the purpose of priming grenades and recognised the same officer as having brought men in to replenish their supply. He wrote:

This Warwicks. officer came off the beach with me in the same RE pontoon in fact, he started to order the chaps in our overcrowded craft to do this, that and the other until he was given the option of shutting up, or swimming for it.

Just before the last of the Battalion had been taken off the beach,

'C' Company (which during the accurate and vicious enemy fire on the 28th had helped the town of Bergues to hold firm) was required to participate further, as part of the rearguard force. However, the Company was later successfully disengaged.

That the 2nd's sister battalions had suffered in giving a valiant account of themselves can be derived from the figures relating to the numbers of men fortunate enough to have been evacuated:

The 1st-7th Battalion had 15 officers and about 220 other ranks left.

The 8th Battalion, only 8 officers and 134 men.

Providentially, not all units were so grievously affected by casualties, or the numbers of those who were safely evacuated from the beaches would not have been so high. Churchill's figure, derived from Admiralty records, is 338,226, including approximately 115,000 French troops.

The evacuation was welcomed with relief by the British, for although the events of Dunkirk were a deliverance rather than a victory, the greater part of the BEF was recovered (less, of course, its equipment), together with a sizeable number of Frenchmen. The implication of the recovery of so many men was a long-term tragedy for the Germans – as General F. Halder feared when, as early as 28th May, he realised that Germany might have to face the recovered Allied forces at some time in the future. Hence, those who called it 'the miracle of Dunkirk' could not be accused of overstatement, whether in regard to the actual evacuation or its long-term effects.

The constituent parts of the miracle as this concerned the actual evacuation, were varied. There was, in the first instance, the overall factor that such a large scale evacuation seemed impossible to the German leaders whose greater concern was with matters other than cutting the Allies off from the one remaining port. The success of Operation Dynamo exceeded the wildest hopes of Churchill who, at one time, 'would not have wagered on more than 50,000 as a maximum'.

Next, there was the incredible decision of Hitler to halt Kleist's Panzer forces on 24th May when they were within reach of Dunkirk. This was taken at a meeting at Charleville on the 24th

May when Hitler, in rejecting the idea of Brauchitsch for a full-scale armoured attack on the 1st Army Group, stated that the forces of the Allied Army were already doomed and that it was of prior importance to prepare for an offensive south of the Somme. He therefore ordered the armoured formations to re-group preparatory to the offensive – and gave the order for the battle in Flanders to be concluded by the Luftwaffe. Hitler was later to state that he did not wish to get his tanks bogged down in the Flanders mud. It would also seem that Göring had pleaded with Hitler for the Luftwaffe to have the honour of administering the *coup de grace*.

Also, Hitler had delegated to Rundstedt the responsibility of deciding whether the advance should be resumed, to the consternation of Brauchitsch who regarded the halt as a stupid decision and to the annoyance of Halder, whose reaction has already been noted.

Then there was bad weather which grounded most of the Luftwaffe and caused Halder to complain that the Germans were compelled to watch countless thousands of the enemy get away to England 'right under our noses'. Breathing space was given to the Allies when, having relented, Hitler ordered on 26th May that the advance towards Dunkirk and Cassel should be renewed – but the order took 16 hours to put into operation as many units were engaged in repair work to vehicles.

Not unimportant was the state of the weather which, though unkind to the Germans in causing their aircraft to be grounded proved excellent for the purposes of the Royal Navy and supporting vessels. The English Channel could hardly ever have so perfectly resembled a mill-pond, so that the men of the Royal and Merchant Navies together with those of the Little Ships, were better able to play their enormous part in the execution of the brilliantly conceived operation. The Royal Air Force, which was much maligned by so many who were unable to see what was being done from the air, had such a significant part to play that Churchill ascribed the gaining of the 'victory inside this deliverance' to the men of the Royal Air Force.

Furthermore, there was the extreme courage of those troops (French, as well as British) whose task was to harry the enemy so as to enable the work of recovery to take place. To many of these men was given an almost suicidal task, which dictated that they should die, or be taken prisoner. Withdrawal to friendly shores was denied to many of these who, as at Wormhout, were required to hold their positions to the last round and the last man.

But the last ships had hardly left Dunkirk when Hitler launched an offensive on France, and for the SS-troops who were involved in the Battle of Wormhout there remained many more miles to be covered. With the fall of Wormhout in the late evening of 28th May, the victorious and chastened Nazis moved on to Calais. Then they participated in the Battle of the Marne, which provided them with what Otto Baum described as 'no serious encounter'. After that, they continued to advance southwards at a rapid pace, taking large numbers of prisoners. On the conclusion of the Armistice with France on 25th June, they were in Clermont-Ferrand and a week later, in the suburbs of Paris. Forbidden to enter the French capital, the *Leibstandarte* marched to Metz and remained there throughout 1940, undergoing training.

CHAPTER TEN

A Sound of Digging

It was the morning of 30th May. Soon, the newly-promoted Commanding Officer and his six platoons would be back in England and though weary, safe and sound. But in Wormhout, the warm sun had dried the churned-up mud of the scarred landscape into hard, irregular ridges. The last sparks had flickered away in the blackened beams of the gutted houses and the few families who had returned to their stark and ransacked homes sat in the entrances, too tearful to be angry.

From the corners of the fields where they had defensively huddled themselves together, the cattle were now spread out in the open, tearing gently at the grass. On the branches of shell-stunted trees birds twittered to the accompaniment of their fellows, perched in bedraggled hedges alongside which an occasional body still lay.

Littered about the countryside and marring the young corn, was the grotesque mess of war. Guns and pouches and bren-carriers and steel helmets. The steel scarecrow of the occasional tank. Gone from the harrowing scene were the participants. The proud *Leibstandarte,* to storm through other fields. The British, some to their island and the less fortunate to prison camps.

But in the Esquelbecq meadow, a little group of severely wounded men hung on to such life as remained in them, inside and near to the corpse-littered barn. For two days they had endured the agony of their wounds and had been granted the blessing of peace only in those moments of unconsciousness which nature kindly lays upon the gravely-ill. Those who were not so blessed, craved and cried out agonisingly for a drink.

Charles Daley lay in the entrance of the building, unable to move. His right leg had been shattered by bullets from an automatic rifle. His left leg was injured, too. It will be recalled that he had also been shot in the shoulder and chest. Weakened and bemused, he watched Privates Bennett and Johnson crawling with considerable difficulty to a nearby ditch in an effort to obtain water. Whether from them or the hands of another, he was not sure, but Daley drank a little and affirmed its taste to be very good.

A farmer came to fetch some milk churns which had been left outside the barn since before the time of the massacre. His arrival filled the wounded men with hope, but his demeanour clearly shewed that he had no intention of becoming involved in a matter which might endanger him. Despite the desperate pleadings of the thirsty and feverish men, he refused to give them a drink and went away.

Having returned from his exhausting journey to the ditch, Jack Bennett (who was gravely wounded in the stomach) lay outside the barn and was seen by a couple of German medical personnel, who had been looking for their own wounded. Being able to speak English, they exchanged words with some of the injured men and Daley received the impression that they were shocked at what had taken place. Departing to obtain an ambulance, the Germans returned within the hour – but were too late to help Bennett, who had already died.

The noise of the ambulance revived Parry, who had been intermittently unconscious during most of the two days. His account of what followed, is compelling:

'I remember coming round and hearing a man crying for his mother. Once, I came round and tried to stand. Somehow, I must have moved a few yards away from the barn in a waking moment which I cannot recall. But when I got to my feet, I was too weak, and couldn't even notice that I had moved into a pile of cow manure and slipping, I fell into it. On two other occasions I rose to my feet, and fell down again.

'Later, I heard a noise which woke me up. Looking across from where I lay, I could see what seemed to be a truck. Moving my head a little higher, which was a great effort, I saw Red Cross markings on the truck. I saw them carrying two fellows out of the barn, and I think I heard some digging. They picked up two more men, and put them on stretchers and as they carried them away, it occurred to me that they had not seen me. Ill though I was, I also realized that I was lying in a particularly bad spot to be detected. I had been blown out of the barn on to a side of the building where the growth was especially high. It may have been tall grass, or weeds. Anyway, it covered me very well and realizing that they could miss me, I tried to shout. 'Opening my mouth – or rather, trying to open it – I found that I couldn't even shout. There was a clot of blood in my mouth, where I had been shot. And I couldn't stand because of the injury to my leg, which occurred when I was sprayed with automatic fire. My other leg was also hurt.

'It was something like a nightmare in which the harder you try to do something, the more difficult it becomes to achieve. I kept on hoping. Hoping that they would look my way – but at the same time, I knew that I was too well hidden for them to catch sight of me.

'Then I had an idea which seemed like a great discovery at the time! It was that if I raised my arm, they might see it. Slowly, I pushed my arm up.

'Fortunately, they saw me – and the one thing which stands out, is that their handling of me was ever so gentle. There were six or seven of us taken from the barn wounded, but alive, thank God. I remember the great feeling of relief which came over me as I was placed in the ambulance. Inside the vehicle, I fell asleep.

'I woke up in a farmhouse and saw what I took to be a French farmer, whose wife was standing by his side. She was trying to feed me with some milk. Afterwards, I remembered a 100-franc note which I had in my pocket. Feeling so grateful, I took it out, and offered it to her. But she wouldn't take it. As she shook her head she was crying, and when she saw that I was becoming upset at her not accepting my gift, she took it.

'I was then taken to Boulogne and from there, to somewhere in Belgium. Later, I went to Stalag 9C.'

Charles Daley lost consciousness as he was being driven from the site of the massacre and recovered to find himself in a field dressing station, where he was treated with kindness. He remembers 'an elderly man with a white beard, who made a note of the statements

I gave him'.

From Boulogne he went to Camiers, where an English surgeon, Major Martin, amputated his leg.

Daley makes no mention of the number of men who were recovered from the barn, but Lavelle says that seven men survived the crime and counts Bennett in this number.

Thus, Parry and Lavelle agree that six or seven men who were seriously wounded were brought out by the Germans and treated with kindness.

It is impossible to say exactly how many men were murdered in the barn, or on the forced march: but a rough calculation can be made after establishing the number of men who escaped, or whose bodies were not buried on the site. It can be determined that the following men survived the massacre:

Evans.

Hall, who escaped alone.

Hopper.

Tombs, Gill, Dutton, Cooper and Box, with the latter shot in the endeavour to break away.

West, who made his way out alone.

Left in the barn, were Daley, Johnson, Kelly, Lavelle, Parry and Townsend. Bennett, who survived for two days was buried on the site. It is possible that Lynn-Allen's body was initially interred in the meadow.

As Box died outside the vicinity of the meadow, he is counted as a survivor of the massacre.

This makes a total of 15 men who are known to have survived.

In his book *The London Cage*, Lieutenant-Colonel A. Scotland states that '60 British soldiers were killed': but on another occasion referred to 'the murder of 80 to 90 prisoners of war'.

Estimates given by the survivors as to how many men were forced into the barn, vary – but all are agreed that the building was filled with men. Captain Lynn-Allen complained that there was not enough room for the wounded to lie down: Evans states that due to the crowded conditions, a small group of men were compelled to stand in the doorway: Hopper says, 'We were forced into the cowshed like sardines'.

The building measured 21 feet by 10 feet 6 inches; and a practical experiment has demonstrated that a building of similar proportions could contain 105 men, plus the four or five in the doorway. In the interests of moderation, one would settle for a round figure of 100 men. Daley says: 'According to my estimate, there were about 90 altogether'. Evans: 'There were 90 to 100, all told.' Lavelle: 'There were nearly 100.'

So, with 15 known survivors, it is not unreasonable to suppose that about 85 men were murdered.

With such a figure in mind, visitors to the Military Cemetery in Esquelbecq will be mystified to discover the graves of no more than 30 men who could have been involved in the massacre. The reasons are several. Within a few days of the men being murdered, a mass grave was opened in the vicinity of the barn for the reception of the bodies. Normally, the officer in charge of the interment would have recorded the names of the dead men on referring to the identity discs on the bodies. But in this case, identity discs had been removed from nearly every prisoner shortly after capture – which would appear to indicate the intentions of the Germans who drove the prisoners into the meadow.

In 1941, the bodies were taken up by local labourers under German supervision; and it is believed that it was considered expedient for some bodies to be re-interred in Esquelbecq, others in Wormhout and the rest, elsewhere. A local official, who prefers to be nameless, informed the author that when the Germans discovered the reason for the existence of the bodies they were anxious to disperse them.

The War Graves Commission did not assume responsibility for maintenance of the Cemetery at Esquelbecq (as this refers to graves of World War II) until 1948, and the graves at Wormhout, in 1947. It was not until some time afterwards that headstones were erected – and because hardly any of the bodies bore marks of identification, the names which are carved on the headstones do not (except by coincidence) relate to the graves which they mark.

All the names which appear on headstones in plot III, row F, at Esquelbecq are unrelated to the bodies underneath, as is obvious from the words 'Buried near this spot'. Such names as do appear, were the result of research based on information supplied by survivors and others who, naturally, could not supply a complete list of those who were in the barn. Hence, at Esquelbecq, 23 stones bear names and 7 do not.

At Wormhout Cemetery, there are 33 burials in rows A, B and D which are classified as 'unknowns'.

The War Graves Commission cannot provide means of identification where none existed at the time of burial, nor can it compute the exact number of interments in relation to which there existed an original laxity.

*

As the survivors were being taken out of the barn at Esquelbecq, two men at Le Paradis (about 20 miles south of Wormhout) had survived a similar massacre and were being tended by a farmer's wife. There was presumed to have been a link between the two outrages, so it is of interest to consider what happened at Le Paradis. Each crime has features in common – even the number of men involved. Also, they were separated in time by one day.

In the early afternoon of 27th May, remnants of the 2nd Battalion, Royal Norfolk Regiment were holding out in a large house in the tiny village. Cut off and lacking ammunition, they decided to surrender. Two or three men emerged from the house holding a white towel in token of surrender, but were shot down. The others, who numbered over 90, came out: and their surrender was accepted by the Germans to the accompaniment of cheers.

Many of the prisoners had been wounded, but despite their condition, were subjected to rough treatment from the boots and rifle-butts of their captors. They had been captured by men of the *SS-Totenkopf* – a sister unit of the *Leibstandarte* – who were enraged because of the heavy losses they had suffered. Also, their Battalion Commander had been killed in action.

After the prisoners had been paraded on the Rue de Paradis, they were marched towards a farm paddock in which was a large barn and as they entered the paddock, several of the men saw two machine-guns which had been placed about 100 yards from the barn. The barrels pointed towards the building; and the line of prisoners, with their hands behind their backs, straggled the length of the barn wall.

Suddenly, the machine-guns opened fire on the prisoners mowing them down from left to right. Those who were further back in the file continued to march into the curtain of bullets . . . Due to the inefficiency of the machine-gunners, quite a number of the British did not die at once: and these were finally despatched by rifle and pistol fire. Bayonets were also used.

A Private Pooley, who had already been wounded in the fighting, was hit by machine-gun bullets: and Private Bill O'Callaghan was also hit. Miraculously, the two men survived and O'Callaghan carried Pooley to the safety of a pig-sty. Eventually, they were discovered by Madame Creton (the farmer's wife) who fed them and treated their wounds.

When the two men discovered that Madame Creton and her son Victor were likely to be detected by the Germans, they gave themselves up to a unit which contained the normal type of German soldier and were sent to a POW camp.

CHAPTER ELEVEN

At Large

George Hall was at large for six days and his most terrifying experience was just after leaving the barn, when after lying in the ditch for about an hour, he heard occasional movements which suggested the presence of Germans in the vicinity, but decided to crawl along the hedge. Eventually he came to some abandoned British equipment and felt grateful that he had reached his own lines; but as he was making for the next point of cover, some Germans spotted him and fired.

Instinctively, he dropped to the ground and though unharmed, decided that his only chance was to pretend that he had been killed. Prostrate, he was sure that the Germans would see him trembling; and as they drew nearer, they actually inspected his body from a distance of about six yards and were satisfied that they had killed him, for they moved off.

He continued to play the part of a corpse until he was sure that it was safe to get up – and when he looked around, it seemed that the whole neighbourhood was empty. Hardly believing his luck, he walked out of Wormhout along the backs of the houses and was surprised to hear no sounds of life. He had no idea where he was going, or in which direction he ought to travel. He 'just kept on walking'.

As he moved along he felt very tired, but his weariness was nothing compared to the hunger he felt. He says, 'I was not just hungry, I was starving – and so, I ate grass. It's hard to believe, but I actually enjoyed it.'

His recollection of his situation at certain times is, naturally, hazy. The six-day period was one long walk during which he was

117

merely anxious to stay alive. On one occasion he came across a
herd of cows, and decided that it ought to be possible to obtain
milk. But he had been brought up in Quarry Bank, where men live
hard but have milk deposited on their doorsteps, in bottles. He was
not without courage, but rural sights were alien to his world, and as
he approached the cows he felt that he would much rather square
up to a heavy-weight boxer than come face-to-face with the horned
creatures. Drawing nearer to the herd, he was amazed that the
animals seemed unconcerned. Emboldened, he crawled underneath what looked to be the likeliest cow and tried to milk her.
'But', he says, 'I hadn't got a clue, and so I never got my drink of
milk.'

Leaving the field, he saw a railway embankment and thought it a
good idea to walk along the track. As he moved along the line, he
saw a distant figure slowly approaching him. For a moment, he was
concerned at meeting someone who could be hostile, but as he
strained his eyes, he saw that it was an old woman carrying a large
bag in each hand.

George felt that she had been shopping, in which case there
would be food in the bags. As he thought of the prospect he could
hardly contain himself, for food was now the stuff of imagination.
But suddenly, he looked at his trousers – and for the first time in
days, realized what an unkempt, unwashed sight he was. His
trousers were badly torn and his singlet was stained with the blood
of the dead man who had collapsed on top of him, in the barn. Running his hand over his cheeks, he felt the evidence of his unshaven
state. Reluctantly, he owned that he must have presented a
frightening sight. And so, despite his consuming hunger, his over-
-riding consideration was for the old woman – and he turned away.

Within the hour he was picked up by a German mobile unit and
placed in a motor-cycle sidecar. On the way, they passed the bodies
of some British soldiers, lying in the ditch. Pointing, the German
who was driving the motor-cycle, shouted, 'Your comrades!'

Arriving at what seemed to be a Transport Unit, Hall met what
he describes as 'My first, good German'. This man said he had
relatives in England and talked about London, which he seemed to
know rather well. Demonstrating his friendliness, he opened tins of

soup and beans and gave Hall his first meal in six days.

He says, 'I enjoyed the grass, but what that German gave me was better than a banquet.'

As the German served the meal his comrades shewed their disapproval, and openly rebuked him. Nevertheless, he continued to look after the English prisoner; and after the meal, took Hall to a nearby stream. Providing soap and a razor, he allowed the prisoner to wash and shave.

Though faced with the prospect of a prison camp, Hall was not sorry. He had not enjoyed the past two weeks, in which the Battalion had suffered the physical and mental strains of war. He had seen many of his friends die in action. He had been without proper food and adequate sleep for longer than he cared to remember. At first hand, he had experienced one of the most cruel events of the war.

A prison camp could hardly be as bad as Tournai, Hollain and Wormhout . . .

Reginald West came nearest to eluding the Germans, remaining at large for over five months, and the story of his experiences after the events in the meadow would provide exciting material for a separate book.

Early in the morning of 29th May, the birds awakened him and as he opened his eyes, he listened carefully before walking over to the window. Peering through the curtains, he saw that the road was deserted and except for the singing of the birds, there was absolute silence. He wondered what had happened to the men who had defended the town, and felt tempted to return to the barn but decided against such a course of action.

The immediate problem was his raging thirst and the pangs of hunger, so he searched the house but of food and drink, he found none. Carefully, he crept out of the back door and saw that other houses were quite near. Searching them he found one crust of bread, which was very stale. Biting on the crust, he sat down to consider the situation and suddenly remembered that there had been clothes in some of the houses; so he decided to get rid of his uniform, if he could find clothes to fit.

With a shirt from one house and trousers and jacket from another, he completed quite a transformation. Placing a beret on his head he surveyed himself in a mirror, and was satisfied with what he saw. His search having yielded no footwear, he was compelled to retain his Army boots.

Feeling quite safe, he walked along the road and was astonished that there was no one in sight. After walking about a mile, he met an old man who told him that the Germans were in occupation of the whole coast, and he congratulated himself that he had changed his clothes. On asking the old man if he had any food, he discovered that he was not the only hungry man in those parts, for the poor old man had not eaten for two days. However, he had some beer in the house and although it was the weakest brew that West had ever tasted, it was a satisfying drink.

Saying goodbye to his host, he moved on. As he walked along he felt that if he was to get back to England, the best idea would be to make for Spain – but he had no map, nor was he sure of the distance involved.

Hungry and footsore, he pressed on and became more and more determined that, no matter how great the distance, or how long it might take, he would get to Spain. Keeping as far as possible to the fields, he managed to avoid nearby villages. For food, he ate raw potatoes and peas.

On the second night, he met up with three men. One was Joe Fagan, a private from his own regiment. The others were, Sergeant Tom Guthrie, of the Argyle and Sutherland Highlanders, and Private Bob Dundas, of the Cameronians. They were as hungry and thirsty as West, and delighted to share his company.

Discussing his idea to make for Spain, they were able to consult a map which Guthrie had, and agreed to make their way to Cete, which they saw was on the border. The idea was to move on to Tangiers, and Gibraltar – and England.

During the next day they were in the region of Arras, and as they walked along searching the gutter for cigarette ends, a horse-drawn cart halted. Inside, was what seemed to be a French farmer and his wife.

Jumping down, the woman queried, 'You are English?' Introducing herself as Madame Meplanse, she said that her husband was a farmer in Hebuterne; and after inviting the men to climb into the cart, she introduced her husband, whose name was Max.

At the farm the men were treated to an excellent meal and supplied with clean clothes. They were assured that they would be perfectly safe, and told to regard the farm as their home for the duration of their stay. It emerged that Madame Meplanse had contacts, and would be arranging for the men to move on when the time was opportune. [1]

The four men worked on the farm and soon became accustomed to their new style of life, working as hard as they could so as to shew their considerable appreciation.

On one occasion, Germans came to inspect the farm and discovered West in the kitchen. Max told them that his companion was one of his labourers. As a result of the inspection, six German sergeants were billeted in the farmhouse – and so well did the 'labourers' play their parts that the Germans shewed no suspicions.

One day, the sergeants left to go on an exercise, and were absent for the greater part of the week. Only two Germans came back. West was told that the others had been killed and that the men who had returned were suffering from burns. The Meplanses were convinced that the exercise was a rehearsal for the proposed invasion of England . . .

During the third week in June, the time became opportune for West and his friends to move on: but when their contacts arrived, it was stressed that the group would have to split up for a short time. Fagan, Guthrie and Dundas were taken to another farm in the vicinity: and West found himself in Saillselle, billeted with a farmer whose name was Marcel Rouselle.

At Saillselle, he lived the double life of farm labourer and resistance worker. The French were quick to seize on his signals experience, and he was able to help in the repair of radio sets. Also, he was frequently called upon to employ his knowledge in the sabotage of telephone lines, and remembers one incident with

[1] After the war, Madame Meplanse was decorated by King George VI for sheltering 72 British soldiers and airmen.

sorrow. He had been asked to disconnect a cable in the region of Arras, but an unfortunate Frenchwoman who happened to be passing through the village was accused of the act of sabotage which West had committed. She was shot within the hour.

After about two months a route was finally organised and once more, he was joined by his three friends. With the exception of an occasion when they managed to jump on a train, the whole of their journey across France was made on foot. Their contacts were with priests, who were links in a well-organised chain. Only occasionally did they sleep indoors. During the greater part of their journey they slept rough, and scavenged for food.

On 20th October, they reached Marseille and began to feel that they had a fair chance of making Oran, but were arrested by gendarmes and taken to Fort St Jean. Here, they were grateful for the help and advice of a Church of Scotland Minister, the Reverend D. Caskie, who was working as a Chaplain to Seamen and, secretly, for the Allied cause. He obtained American papers for the men, so as to enable them to be treated as internees, and also contacted their relatives.[2]

In January, they were transferred to St Hippolyte, where they remained for nearly a year. On 17th March 1942, they were taken to Fort de la Revère (Nice). In the September they arrived at Camp de Chambaran (Isère) and, having been declared Prisoners of War, were taken by the Italians to PG 73, Boogna.

When Italy capitulated the Camp was ringed with German parachutists – and the inmates were moved to Stalag 4B, arriving on 24th September 1943.

[2] See p. 130

CHAPTER TWELVE

Faded Swastikas

When the Franco-German armistice was signed on 22nd June 1940, the *Leibstandarte* had penetrated further south than any other German unit and although the German Army could scarcely refer to their existence, the contribution of SS-troops had been considerable. This brought forth tributes from Hitler, who recognized their efforts with suitable decorations; and, though the Führer ostensibly discouraged the growth of Himmler's *Verfügungstruppe*, a new Waffen-SS Division was created.

From the ranks of Nazi supporters in the occupied countries volunteers came forward for the Waffen-SS; and by December 1940, regiments from Denmark and Norway (*Nordland*) and Holland and Belgium (*Westland*) were incorporated into a new division, the 5th SS-Panzerdivision *Wiking*. Its third regiment was provided by the transfer of *Standarte Germania*.

Despite official assurances that the Waffen-SS was not intended to be a purely military force, its strength in 1941 was over double that of the previous year. In March, it had 4 Divisions – *Das Reich*, *Totenkopf*, *Polizei*, and *Wiking*: 2 Brigades – *Leibstandarte* (now increased from Regimental strength) and *Nord*: and an infantry Regiment.

In the spring of 1941, SS-troops were moved to positions along the borders of Russia, along with the greater part of the German Army; but the poor showing of the Italian Army in its ill-advised attack on Greece, together with troubles in the Balkans, led to a short campaign which caused the postponement of the attack on Russia.

In the offensive, which began on 6th April, the *Leibstandarte* went through Serbia into Albania, and stormed through Thessaly. In this campaign, Wilhelm Mohnke was wounded in the foot and the limb had to be amputated. During the time he was becoming accustomed to the wearing of an artificial foot, he was placed in command of the Gross Lichterfelde Barracks, Berlin.

For the attack on Russia, which commenced on 22nd June 1941, the *Leibstandarte* and *Wiking* were placed in Army Group 'A', and the *Leibstandarte* spearheaded the offensive, reaching the coast of the Black Sea in August 1941. By November, the progress made was such that Rostov was taken, but with the onset of winter the tanks became bogged down in the mud, the attack came to a halt – and the Russian resistance began to stiffen.

In December, 100 Russian Divisions were unleashed on the 200-mile front forward of Moscow, and with such effect that the Germans never fully recovered. Overwhelmed by superior numbers, the *Leibstandarte* was cut to ribbons when Rostov was retaken by the Russians in late November. The German Generals appealed to Hitler for permission to withdraw to a milder zone for the winter, but were ordered to hold firm – with the result that the Germans were mown down in large numbers.

In the autumn of 1942 the *Leibstandarte, Das Reich* and *Totenkopf* were withdrawn to France, so as to be fitted with tanks as Panzergrenadiers and return to the thick of the fighting. On their return, the three 'Divisions' were formed into the first SS-Corps and participated in some bitter fighting at Kharkov – which the Russians abandoned on 14th March. Losses on each side were heavy, with the Russians leaving over 20,000 dead on the battlefield and the SS-Corps suffering some 12,000 casualties.

July 1943 saw the assault on the Kursk salient, with the Germans committed to attacking a virtually impregnable position. The Waffen-SS units distinguished themselves in a hopeless situation, with the result that Hitler decided to add to the number of their Divisions; and in October, the *Leibstandarte* was re-mustered as a Panzer-division. To this end, it was transferred to Belgium in 1944 for re-equipment and re-inforcement.

Waffen-SS units were particularly barbarous in their treatment of Russian prisoners, and were themselves to complain concerning the Russian methods of dealing with their prisoners! One such complaint concerned the murder of six members of the *Leibstandarte* Three Company, and it was obvious that the SS had encountered a foe whose brutality could match their own. It became expedient to call a halt to such barbarity as existed in SS-units: and Dietrich is on record as saying that 'We owe it to the title on our sleeves . . . ' [1]

During the Russian campaign Dietrich was brought back by Hitler from his command of the 1st Armoured Corps, to perform an intriguing task. This was connected with the overthrow of Mussolini and his subsequent imprisonment on the summit of Gran Sasso d'Italia, in the Abruzzi Appenines. German glider troops rescued the Duce and carried him away to Lake Garda, where he was guarded by a detachment of the *Leibstandarte*. Dietrich's mission involved the safe conduct of Mussolini's mistress, Clara Petacci, back to the arms of the fallen dictator, the Führer apparently being concerned that the Duce should be comforted.

After the Allied landings in Normandy during 1944, the SS-Divisions were again thrown into the thick of the fight. The *Leibstandarte* was engaged in the Caen area, where in the Odon battle the *Leibstandarte, Hohenstauffen,* and *Hitler Jugend* halted the attempt of the Allied armies to break out of the Caen pocket and the offensive was haited. This particularly nasty collection of Nazi youths was suitably to distinguish itself by committing the first atrocities of the campaign. These involved the murder of over 50 Canadian troops, in small and large groups, after being captured by the *Jugend*.

These teen-aged brutes were also responsible for the callous murder of civilians, including children.

In July, an unspeakably inhuman outrage was committed by other 'élite' troops of the *Das Reich*, which was moving north from Bordeaux when it encountered the attention of resistance fighters, and the advance was slowed down. Halting at Oradour-sur-Glane, reprisals were inflicted on the whole population. After the men of the town had been shot, the women and children were herded into

[1] *The Order of the Death's Head*, p. 433

the Church, which was set on fire. Out of 642 inhabitants, one escaped . . .

When the Americans broke through the Germans' defences in Normandy, speeding southwards, the end was near for the Germans. The last great attack of the SS was entrusted to 'Sepp' Dietrich, who was now in command of the 6th SS-Panzer Army, consisting of: *Leibstandarte, Hitler Jugend, Das Reich* and *Hohenstauffen.* With the 5th Panzers guarding its flank, Dietrich's army had the task of breaking through to Antwerp.

During this offensive, which met with stern resistance from the Americans, the *Leibstandarte* reacted typically when 90 American prisoners were brutally machine-gunned in a meadow outside Malmedy, by Obersturmbannführer Jochen Peiper's men.

Already facing defeat in Normandy, Hitler withdrew his SS-Divisions into Hungary, where the last supplies of natural oil were threatened by the advance of the Russians, who had overwhelmed Budapest. Though fighting with spirit, Dietrich's 6th Army was forced to acknowledge the superior numbers of the Russians, being driven back into Vienna in the late March of 1945.

Hitler vented his spleen on his beloved Waffen-SS, and to his loyal Dietrich he ordered Keitel to send the message: 'The Führer believes that the troops have not fought as the situation demanded and orders that the SS-Divisions *Adolf Hitler, Das Reich, Totenkopf* and *Hohenstauffen* be stripped of their arm-bands.' Dietrich responded by sending for his Divisional Commanders and, throwing the message on the table, shouted, 'That's all the thanks you get for all you've done in the last five years.' He is also purported to have replied to Hitler that rather than obey such an order, he would shoot himself. In addition, he threatened to send his decorations back.

Wilhelm Mohnke was spared the desperate fighting in Hungary due to his being posted to Berlin for appointment as Commandant of the Reich Chancellery Defence, with the rank of Brigadeführer. Here, fate was to link him with Wormhout, for working in the transport section of the Chancellery, was Werner Ritter, the Seven Company guard who was wounded in the barn incident . . .

In the bunker, Mohnke was afforded the unenviable opportunity

Reginald West, 'HQ' Signals

William Cordrey

On the Dunkirk beaches

Wilhelm Mohnke in the late 1930s (left) and in 1988.

After the dedication of the Memorial at Esquelbecq *Left to right* : Albert Evans, J. Lavelle, Alfred Tombs, Charles Daley.

of close contact with the Führer during the period of his decline. As Mohnke watched the frantic comings and goings of the last, eventful weeks, he no doubt recalled the great days when the boots of his comrades had proudly stamped on the ground which was now above his head.

At the end, it was Mohnke who ordered the bunker to be set on fire and afterwards he escaped with the first group which was ordered to leave. Fleeing from the fire of a Russian tank, the party was driven underground at the Maikaefer Barracks, and after a few hours hid in a cellar in the Schoenhäuser Allee. The Russians captured the party on 2nd May.

Mohnke became a pawn in the hands of the Russians, who found it convenient to withhold information concerning him from the Germans and the Allies. Consequently, many were led to suppose that he had ended his life along with three others who, during the last conference in the bunker, had affirmed a determination to commit suicide.

CHAPTER THIRTEEN

The Story Told

In a Military Cemetery of World War I, there is a headstone on which is carved the sad speculation 'We often wonder how you died . . .' Unfortunately, many servicemen died in circumstances which make it impossible for anyone to know the details. Often, there were no witnesses to acts of heroism, or self-sacrifice performed but a few moments before the end. Similarly, the stark adjective 'missing' which appeared on letters addressed to countless relatives, was so inconclusive as to lead them to hope for better news to follow.

After the evacuation of Dunkirk, many thousands of relatives were quickly informed of the safe arrival of their loved ones in the Channel Ports. But there were others who heard nothing for many weeks – and when the fateful letter arrived, its message was often inconclusive.

When May Tombs realized that her husband had not been brought back to England she was absolutely sure, despite the absence of information, that he was alive. 'He promised me', she says: 'that he would come back, and I believed him.' For several months she could rely only upon her husband's promise, and continued in hope even on receipt of an official letter couched in frozen language, which stated that as from a certain date, her Army allowance would be changed for a widow's pension.

Kathleen West also received the usual, cold communications and decided that she would seek a more personal message, even if unhopeful. By bus she travelled to Warwick where the Barracks was situated, and where some of her husband's comrades lived. Calling at the office and knocking many doors, her mission was unfruitful;

and so, on her return, she wrote a letter to the Commanding Officer.

His reply reads:

Dear Madam,

I am in receipt of your enquiry dated 29th September 1940 in respect of your husband. I have interviewed Sergeant Underhay and he made the following statement:-

'Private West was telephone operator with battalion headquarters. I was near him constantly whilst the battle was on. Towards the end of the morning I was in the next trench to him and saw him occasionally, still looking after the telephone. I was wounded and left that area with the last party. We had been split up and I am not sure if Private West was still there or whether he had endeavoured to get away. It is possible that he was taken prisoner, as other men in the same group have since been notified as prisoners.'

Every endeavour is being made to get information about men of the battalion and I trust that some news of your husband will soon come to light.

A large number of soldiers believed killed have since been reported prisoners of war.

Yours sincerely,
P. Hicks,
Lt-Colonel.

Though its contents were vague, Mrs West's hopes were undiminished. 'We were married', she says, 'in St Paul's, Hampstead, Birmingham, on a Wednesday. During all the time Reginald was away, Wednesday became a special day on which I would go into the Church, to pray. Not once did I doubt that my prayers would be unanswered. Always, I trusted that God would bring him back to me . . .'

The first indication of her husband's whereabouts came with a letter from a surprising source. It was headed 'The Church of Scotland Overseas Committee', signed by the general secretary and dated 28th November. Referring to the work of the Reverend Caskie in Marseille, it went on:

> ... he adds that there is no cause for anxiety unless I hear from him to the contrary, and he asks me to inform relatives and friends at home that their men-folk cannot send word from Marseille except through him, and that by telegram only.
>
> The foregoing will relieve your mind, for I am sure you may have been wondering why direct news has not reached you. You may, of course, still continue to send an occasional short telegram or letter – about once a month, but not oftener – and you have most carefully to observe not to indicate, either in the address, or in the communication itself, the fact of anyone connected with you being a serviceman, nor should there be any enclosures, and no reference of any kind made to the war, or war affairs. I would also ask you to observe most carefully that you should regard any information I have sent you as *strictly confidential*, not to be made public, or discussed with outsiders, and kindly note to use the address *exactly* as I give it – Care Reverend Caskie, 26, Rue de Forbin, Marseille. Use no contractions like c/o for 'care', or 'Rev' for Reverend, and do not put on the word, 'France'. . . .

In April 1941, she received another letter from the same office informing her that Reginald had been moved to St Hippolyte, that the food there 'is sufficient and good', and that the place was about 100 kilometres north-west of Marseille.

Many relatives of men who were in similar circumstances have cause to be grateful to those who, like Mr Caskie, placed themselves in situations of jeopardy, for no reward except that of serving their fellow-creatures. It becomes a salutary exercise to compare the friendliness of the communications from such sources with those which emanated from official quarters, and couched in dead-pan officialese.

One untidily duplicated and shoddily constructed letter which Mrs West received from Whitehall, must have caused many other wives ruefully to question the gratitude of the nation in its bland

notification of the miserable pittance which became due on account
of men 'reported missing and of whom no news has unfortunately
been received': in KathleenWest's case, her allowance was 15/6 per
week . . .

In October 1943, a large number of men returned to Great Britain as the result of a prisoner-exchange with Germany. Nearly all
had been incapacitated in some way, and repatriated with them
were three or four survivors of the massacre. Many were in need of
medical attention, so that it was necessary for them to be admitted
into hospital.

Richard Parry has an interesting souvenir of his return. Printed
on war-time paper, it is the menu of a 'Welcome Home Supper'
which was held at 110 Convalescent Depot, Glencourse:-

>Cream of Potato Soup
>Cold Sirloin of Beef
>York Ham
>Ox Tongue
>*Salads*: Eggs, Tomato, Lettuce, Winter Salad,
>Russian Salad
>
>---
>
>Creamed mashed potatoes
>Brussels sprouts
>
>---
>
>Apple Tart, with Cream
>Mince Pies
>Fresh Fruit
>
>---
>
>Coffee
>Beer
>Minerals
>Cigarettes

In the treatment of its returned heroes the nation had at least
begun well.

The return of Charles Daley was noted by the *Sunday Pictorial*, which considered his re-union with his dog worthy of a full-page spread. Underneath a photograph of him dressed in uniform and holding a stick, the caption read:

This is the day they've been waiting for.
The boss is back and they're off for a walk together again. Boss, is Private Charles Daley, of Chelsea, who has been repatriated from a German Prison Camp. And the Alsatian is 'Bob', who has been cared for since Dunkirk by the Blue Cross Kennels, where this grand re-union picture was taken.

The attention which Fleet Street paid to Bert Evans resulted in the wrath of officialdom being brought down upon his head, when a journalist was sent from London to Southampton for the purpose of obtaining an 'I-was-there' type of story. Evans told her about Wormhout, and on the following day, the account appeared on the front page of a National newspaper. As Evans had not been interviewed by the appropriate military authority, he was severely censured on account of his misdemeanour.

It is quite likely that the unintentional and premature leaking of the story assisted the official assimilation of it; for Private Pooley, who was wounded in the Le Paradis massacre and repatriated at the same time as Evans, failed to convince his interviewers of the veracity of his tale. Indeed, the story of the Le Paradis massacre might never have been brought to the light of day, nor would the culprit have been brought to justice, but for the dogged persistence of Pooley in the face of the 'but-the-Germans-didn't-behave-like-that attitude.[1]

Ironically, whereas the Wormhout story seems to have been accepted readily and the tale of Le Paradis was not, the evil genius of the Le Paradis crime was punished, but the culprits of Wormhout went scot free.

However, those who sought that the guilty men of Wormhout should be brought to justice began well, so that towards the end of 1943 the three returned survivors received letters promising that the

[1] The general behaviour of the German army was, indeed, fair: but the massacre at Le Paradis was perpetrated by the SS.

criminals would be sought and put on trial. As Richard Parry kept
all the correspondence leading up to the interrogation of a number
of Germans, it is possible to follow the events as seen through his
eyes.

The first letter was from Lieutenant-Colonel H. V. Kendall
(Royal Warwickshire Regiment), and is reproduced in full:

16th December, 1943

Dear Parry,

I have heard recently that you have been repatriated, and also
that you were among the prisoners who were murdered and left
for dead after capture in a barn near Wormhout, on 27th May
1940.[2]

I have already obtained from two members of the Royal
Warwickshire Regiment various statements regarding this incident . . . and I would like any information which you can give
me.

We are very keen to put together a completely authenticated
case, supported by the statements of witnesses, so that we can
send it to the War Office, with the request that it be noted with a
view to some form of punishment being meted out to those
responsible after the war.

I am told that there were from 80 to 120 persons in this barn,
that they were mostly Royal Warwickshire Regiment, but there
were a few gunners and Cheshires; also that the Boche took men
outside in batches of five and shot them, that they threw
grenades into the barn in order to kill off the remainder, and then
came into the barn and sprayed the bodies with Tommy guns.

During this, a Captain Lynn-Allen escaped from the barn,
together with a Private Evans, whom I have interviewed. Captain
Lynn-Allen was actually killed only a short distance away from
the barn, but Evans, although left for dead, survived.

On behalf of the Colonel of the Regiment, I should be very
much obliged if you could see your way to putting the facts as
you know them on paper and sending them to me, and if there

[2] The date was, of course, May 28th: but this mistake was to be repeated by
others.

are any particular remarks which you have to make or anything which you remember Captain Lynn-Allen or anyone else said or did, I should be very much obliged if you would let me have them.

With best wishes and the congratulations of the Regiment on your own escape from such a terrible fate.

Yours sincerely

M. H. V. Kendall.

Lt. Col.

On receiving Parry's reply, Kendall wrote: 'Thank you for your useful letter. It contains much information to confirm the story as put forward by Daley and others, and I am very grateful to you for giving me so many details.'

On 12th February 1944, Parry, who had returned to his home in Llandudno, received a letter from the War Office. This referred to the information he had supplied, and asked if he could recall 'that any of the following were among the victims'. There followed a list of nine names of men from the 2nd Battalion, and two from the Cheshire Regiment, 'B' Company.

In March, a communication arrived from the Treasury solicitor, requesting him to swear an affidavit at Messrs Porter & Co. (Solicitors) Llandudno.

When two years went by with no further information as to how the matter was proceeding, Parry imagined that the enquiry was closed. By this time he was training as a Veterinary Surgeon at Liverpool University and, in any case, immersed in his studies. But on 13th March 1946 he was interested in the contents of a letter from the Judge Advocate General, which read:

German War Crimes

Massacre at Wormhout 27th/28th May, 1940

1. You will remember that you swore an affidavit about this massacre before a Commissioner for Oaths in the Treasury Solicitor's Office in March 1944. Investigations have been proceeding since then and it is now thought that there is a

reasonable chance of finding and punishing at least some of those responsible for the crime.

2. Will you please let me know whether you would be able to identify any of the Germans who took part in the Massacre and whether you would be willing to come to London for this purpose. Your travelling expenses would, of course, be paid and you would be given reasonable remuneration for any financial loss incurred.

3. Please let me have this information as soon as you can, by return if possible, so that I may pass it on to the officer who is at present in Germany investigating this crime.

Meanwhile, Gill, Lavelle and Tombs had returned home and were added to the list of those whose statements were requested; but the official list was by no means complete and presumably, on account of certain names not having been supplied, or sought.

There followed a long period during which nothing more was heard and Evans, Parry and Daley (who received their first letters in 1943) felt sure that the investigations had lapsed. This was by no means the case, for the staff of the War Crimes Interrogation Unit were involved in lengthy and painstaking enquiries, which took them into France and Germany.

In view of the enormity of the task which faced them, they were remarkably successful.

Then, in April 1947, Parry received a letter from the Judge Advocate General's Office:

You will remember that you wrote to me in March last year stating that you were willing to come to London for the purpose of trying to identify some of the Germans who took part in the massacre, or who were responsible for it.

Will you please let me know at your earliest convenience when it would be possible for you to come to London for this purpose . . . the week after next would probably be the most suitable from our point of view.

The next letter read:

I shall be grateful if you will come to London on Tuesday, 22nd April 1947 and, on arrival, proceed to the London District Prisoner of War Cage: 6/7, Kensington Palace Gardens, Bayswater, W8., and report to the Commanding Officer, Lieutenant-Colonel A. Scotland, OBE.

Other survivors received similar instructions, and Bert Evans remembers ' . . . being told that there were supposed to have been four Germans on the identification parade, but that due to one having garotted himself, there would now be three.[3] They were brought in to me on two separate occasions. First, they were wearing civilian clothing; and next, they wore uniform similar to that worn when they were in France.

'I only recognized one of the men. I remembered him well from the barn incident, because he was so much taller than the other guards and had a sabre scar on his cheek. But I was not able to say if he had thrown a grenade, or fired a weapon; and I was not going to say that he had done something of which I was not a witness. Anyway, he was certainly there, on that day . . . '

On 14th April a letter went out from Colonel Scotland:

1. Investigations in the above case have now reached the stage where it has become necessary for the undermentioned to proceed to Wormhout and to the scene of the crime:

            Albert Evans
            Charles Edward Daley
            Richard Tudor Parry
            Albert Montague

2. The purpose of the visit will be to reconstruct the various locations and positions at and near Wormhout in the morning, afternoon and evening of the 28th May 1940.

3. The party will be away for three days. Two days will be sufficient to proceed to Wormhout and carry out the necessary investigations there, whilst a third day is being set aside for your

---

[3] The records of the General Register Office shew no entry relative to the death of any ex-SS guard in custody at the time.

convenience, to enable you to reach London. The party will proceed by car from London . . .'.

So, on 6th June, the four men arrived in Wormhout, accompanied by Major T. Pantcheff and RSM Stanton, of the War Crimes Interrogation Unit. Details of the Company and other locations were obtained, as these related to before and during the Battle of Wormhout. Movements of the prisoners' parties were traced, and the events at the barn were reconstructed.

Evans remembers that during the reconstruction of the massacre, Parry insisted he was the last man to enter the barn, prior to pushing through to the back. Also, he recalls the reconstruction of the scene which involved Parry lying with his legs inside, and the top part of his body outside the barn. Whilst Parry lay in his position, Montague was asked to stand at the point where the first group of five men were shot; and Evans was placed where the second group died – and it was confirmed that, as Parry lay with his legs inside the barn (which, at that time was still standing) each point could clearly be seen.[4]

The sequence of events was agreed as:
(a) The throwing of grenades and small arms fire.
(b) The forcing out of the two groups of five men.
(c) The shooting of those in the barn who were still alive.
(d) The shot which entered Parry's mouth.

Montague, who was not involved in the Massacre, was able to give positions and details of the group of prisoners captured after 1700 hours.

With a number of points settled, a clearer picture of the events of 28th May emerged, and the party returned to England to await further developments.

[1] See sketch, p.138

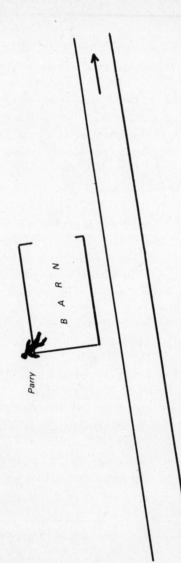

First group of
five men were shot here.

B A R N

Parry

Second group of
five men were shot here

● From his position where he had been blown partly through the barn, Parry was able to witness the murders of the two groups of five prisoners.

● When investigations were being made after the war on the site of the massacre, Montague was posted on the site of the first shooting and Evans on that of the second, and so established that it was possible for Parry to have witnessed each shooting.

CHAPTER FOURTEEN

Power of an Oath

When Colonel Scotland studied the papers relating to the Wormhout massacre he was not surprised to learn that the Germans who were alleged to have participated in the crime were members of the *Leibstandarte*. Already, he was in possession of much information regarding Hitler's favourite SS-Panzerdivision, for towards the end of 1944, he had been requested to assist a Commission of Enquiry set up to investigate atrocities committed against Canadian troops in the same year.

The crimes were those which occurred in the Caen area perpetrated by the *Hitler Jugend*, with prisoners executed in brutal circumstances and, in many cases, as the result of direct orders.

So, when Scotland came to investigate the events which took place at Esquelbecq, in 1940, he was not surprised that the subject of his investigations was 'The murder of 80 or 90 British prisoners of war by members of the German Armed Forces at Wormhout (France) on 28th May 1940.'

He looked forward to his interview with 'Sepp' Dietrich, for he had heard much about him, and remembered his involvement in the Röhm Purge executions which took place at Stadelheim Prison, in 1943.

He recalled that the Nazi was already in custody for his part in the murder of American soldiers during the Battle of the Bulge in 1944.

Stripped of his power and denied the privilege of rank, Dietrich revealed 'a miserable wreck of a personality during his interrogation'.[1] As he excused himself of all guilt in connection with the massacre, Hitler's favourite General could only wail that he had spent the day in a ditch, which protest he repeated again and again.

'I know nothing of any shootings', he complained.[2]

As Scotland was to discover (from the corroboration of Alfred Ebner, whose story of his posting to the *Leibstandarte* has already been told),[3] Dietrich had been hiding in the ditch before and during the time of the massacre, and was telling the truth. But that he knew nothing of the affair was a deliberate lie – for Scotland was to discover that, subsequent to the crime, he invoked the SS-oath on his officers.

Significantly, Ebner's statement mentioned conversations which took place between the officers on the evenings on 28th and 29th May, when there was talk of a group of British prisoners, numbering about 70, who were all 'finished off . . .'. Ebner presumed that they had been shot, and claimed to have felt depressed about the story.

A man so obviously possessed of a conscience was out of place in the company of the men of Hitler's favourite regiment.

Rottenführer Schauff was one of the Seven Company guards involved in the incidents leading up to the massacre, and was able to remember 28th May as the day his Battalion Commander (Shützeck) was wounded. He told of helping to capture about 40 prisoners as his platoon moved from the Cassel Road into Wormhout. These were the men to whose party Parry was joined.

He alleged that on arrival at HQ, an SS-officer came out and reprimanded Untersturmführer Heinrich in the presence of his platoon, for 'bringing in prisoners, contrary to orders'. This was the incident to which Parry referred, when he mentioned 'an SS-officer who wore a soft, peaked cap and seemed a big noise'.

After about half-an-hour, Schauff said, Heinrichs came out of the German HQ with eight guards from Eight Company and told him that the said guards knew what to do. Schauff asked where they

[1] *The London Cage*, p. 94

[2] Ibid p. 94

[3] See p. 96 of this book

were going, and was told that the prisoners were to be shot.
Heinrichs had to go back to the Company, but before leaving said
that he was not happy about what was going to be done. On hearing this, the men of Eight Company replied that they would have
no hesitation in carrying out their orders.

Schauff and the three other men from his platoon were ordered to
accompany the party.

In five expressive words, Schauff described the forced march to
the meadow: 'We ran across the fields.'

He alleged that the prisoners were forced into the barn by the
guards of Eight Company, and described the positions of all the
Germans who guarded the barn. He claimed to have taken no part
in the massacre, and related the following:

He and his comrades stood facing the long side of the building, in
the order: Ritter, Schauff, Dorn, Scheide. The other Germans faced
the doorway, and were on Schauff's right.

When some prisoners (Lynn-Allen and Evans) were seen to be
escaping, one of the Eight Company guards opened fire. In the line
of fire, was Ritter, who immediately screamed. Moving over,
Schauff saw that he had been shot through the chest and in the
jaw.[4]

Immediately, Schauff ran for an ambulance, and sped back to
the meadow. Placing the vehicle on the field path, he was assisted
by Dorn in carrying the injured man to the ambulance.

On arrival at HQ, Schauff reported Ritter's wounding to Otto
Baum and diffidently mentioned what was going on in the barn.
The impassive Baum shewed no reaction, but ordered Schauff and
Dorn back to their platoon.

He expressed remorse for what had been done, adding that his
comrades of Seven Company had disapproved of 'the horrible deed
from the beginning.'

Schauff's statement implies that Untersturmführer Heinrichs
and Dorn would have made useful witnesses, but each was killed in
Russia.

---

[4] See sketch of barn incident, p.142

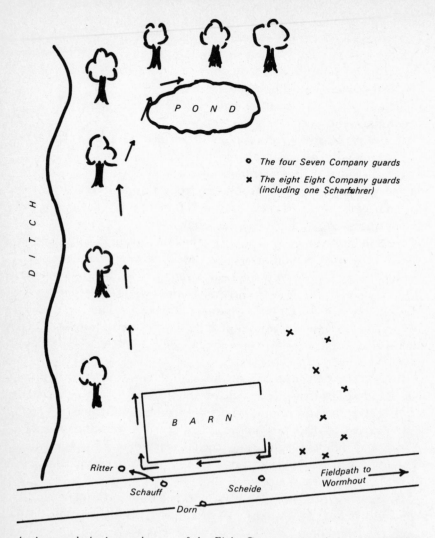

1. A grenade is thrown by one of the Eight Company guards.
2. Lynn-Allen & Evans dash from the barn entrance to the pool (as shewn by arrows), whilst the Germans take cover.
3. A guard of Eight Company fires at the two prisoners with a revolver. The shots miss the prisoners, but wound Ritter, who falls to the ground.
4. Schauff moves over to assist Ritter and runs for the ambulance.
5. Lynn-Allen and Evans reach the pool hide in the water.
6. Schauff returns with ambulance and, together with Dorn, takes Ritter to the HQ. The three men do not return, so participate no further in massacre.

The only other guards held by the Interrogation Unit, were
SS-Rottenführer Koriaka and SS-Oberschütze Schmidt, of Eight
Company.

Each denied being present at the scene of the massacre.

Both men admitted being members of a prisoner escort on 28th
May, but asserted that their duties were quite normal and unmarked by incident.

Their reference to other escort duties being normal was true, but
these concerned the party which contained Montague and Tomes:
it being submitted by Scotland that the two men were in both incidents, and that they deliberately sought to confuse the two parties.

Koriaka claimed that his only knowledge of prisoners being killed was derived from a story he had heard, concerning a number of
men who had been shot attempting to escape . . .

The account of the escaping prisoners was an echo of the official
excuse which, after being concocted, winged its way through the
ranks of the *Leibstandarte*, as emerges from:

Firstly, Otto Baum said that it had been reported to him during
the night of the 28th, or on the next day, that SS-Rottenführer
Linkenhell was marching with his prisoners when one of the British
threw a grenade, and another fired a pistol. The prisoners
scattered, whereupon the escorting Germans fired, with some of the
prisoners being killed and others getting away. During this incident, Ritter was wounded.

Baum did not interrogate Linkenhell at the time, because he was
'too busy'. He reported the matter to Mohnke, who acknowledged
it.

Secondly, SS-Untersturmführer Hasenwinkel, of Seven Company, said that he heard in the evening of the 28th, that a group of
prisoners was en route with an escort, when 'suddenly, the
prisoners threw a grenade'. There was a fight, during which many
prisoners died. He remembered the name of Ritter, and that he had
been wounded in the incident. He recalled no report having been
made, but said that it was possible that Baum reported the matter
to Battalion HQ. As the attack had come from the prisoners, it was
felt that no injustice had been done.

Thirdly, Karl Kummert, of Seven Company, heard that Ritter was wounded by British prisoners whom he was taking to the collecting station. As a result, prisoners were shot.

In support of the story that Ritter had been wounded by shots fired by the British prisoners, it was variously stated that this must have been the case, because German other ranks were not issued with pistols. But the Interrogation Unit traced the *Leibstandarte*'s armourer, who stated that it was not impossible for a German NCO to possess a pistol.

Not the least of Colonel Scotland's difficulties was connected with several important witnesses having been killed in Russia. In addition to Heinrichs and Dorn, Linkenhell fell in the Eastern campaign. Furthermore, it was impossible to cut through the web of lies which had been carefully woven in 1940.

Schauff's statement was useful only insofar as it exonerated him from any part in the massacre, for he was not present at the scene of the crime after Ritter's wounding.

Nor were the British survivors able positively to identify any of the men who were brought before them as having been involved in the massacre. Recalling the invitation to attend the London Cage, Tombs says that he felt bound to decline, because 'looking back, I saw no reason why I should try to identify men who all looked the same in their helmets. Their physical characteristics seemed so similar, for all were tall and of smart appearance'.

Although Evans was able to identify one of the men, like Schauff he was present only at the beginning of the massacre.

Regrettably, Scotland's investigations had proved fruitless. He had scoured Germany for members of the *Leibstandarte* who had been present at Wormhout, some of whom he felt sure knew about the crime but they strenuously denied this. He was convinced that one stumbling block which stood in the way of truth stemmed from the action of Dietrich, who, on learning of the massacre, had invoked the SS-oath. All officers and men were sworn to silence, and the power of the oath survived the War. No oathbreaker could feel safe for the rest of his life.

He had two men in custody whose personal responsibility could not be proved. He wrote:

> We had the grim accounts of the survivors. We had the inade-
> quate stories told by our captive Germans . . . I failed to obtain
> anything of value that might lead to identification of the guilty
> party. In short, I had no case to present to Court.[5]

In the course of the investigation, he had felt that:

> The SS-*Totenkopf* murders of the Royal Norfolk prisoners on the
> previous day, 27th May, had been the subject of chit-chat which
> went over the air from the *Totenkopf* signals branch to the signals
> of the *Leibstandarte*, their sister-unit at Wormhout.

He was frustrated by the unavailability of Mohnke, but it was
unlikely that Mohnke would have been more informative than the
Germans already in custody, for the SS-oath was no less binding
upon him, and of the power of that oath, Scotland had justly
complained. Also, fate had intervened to eliminate Heinrichs, whose
testimony would have been invaluable, for he was inside the German
Battalion HQ when the order for disposal of the prisoners was
issued.

The statements of survivors make it clear that German brutalities
were not confined to the barn incident, but occurred in different
places throughout the morning and afternoon, until 1700 hours.
Each of the following was committed *before* Mohnke assumed Command of the *Leibstandarte*'s 2nd Battalion:–

(a) The shooting of Daley, at the time of his capture.

(b) The murder of about 15 prisoners, witnessed by Evans.[6]

(c) The killing of four men in a petrol-soaked vehicle, which

---

[5] Ibid p. 95

[6] This incident was also related to the author by an official of the Esquelbecq Council,
and is purported to have occurred because the men were found being sheltered by
a French farmer, who was exceedingly fortunate to escape being shot with the British.
All farms were vacated by 1400 hours.

SS-men set on fire.[8] The bodies were seen by Tombs, shortly after capture – and some time before Mohnke became C.O.

It follows that SS-brutality was rife in the ranks of Hitler's favourite regiment at Wormhout, and if there was an individual laden with responsibility, then, despite his protestations, Dietrich was that man. He seemed to appreciate this himself, for after submitting that he had been absent during the greater part of the day when hiding in the ditch, he added: 'It is clear to me, however, that the Commander is responsible for the actions and conduct of his Regiment.'

Even the return to normal prisoner-of-war treatment after 1700 hours seems connected with Dietrich's acute sense of self-preservation, for it was at around 1700 hours that he was recovered from his hiding place. It is not too much to suppose that on his return to his Headquarters, he was informed of the incidents which took place in the meadow. The statement supplied by Ebner mentions that the relationship between Dietrich and his Divisional Commander, was not good. The SS-oath was invoked with Dietrich's superiors in mind, rather than a post-war investigation. At the same time, instructions no doubt went out that there had to be a return to treatment of prisoners which was consistent with the official line.

On 16th May 1946, the Allied War Crimes Commission presented 74 men of the *Leibstandarte* for trial in Dachau. Each was accused of participation in the murder of 129 American prisoners at Malmedy, on 17th December 1944, and among the accused was 'Sepp' Dietrich.

In evidence, Dietrich stated that at a conference with Hitler, on 11th December 1944: 'The Führer said we would have to act brutally and show no inhibitions. He also said that a wave of fright and terror should precede the attack and that the enemy resistance was to be broken by terror.' At a conference with his Commanders on the following day, Dietrich was asked regarding the disposal of prisoners. He replied: 'Prisoners? You know what to do with them.'[9]

[8] *The London Cage*, p. 97
[9] *Massacre at Malmedy*, p. 215

Pressed as to the precise meaning of his ambiguous remark, Dietrich replied that he had meant that the Hague Convention was to be respected. Germany had been a signatory party to the Convention, whose rules state: 'It is forbidden to kill or wound an enemy, who having laid down his arms, or having no longer means of defence, has surrendered at discretion' – Rule 23 (c): 'It is forbidden to declare that no quarter will be given' – Rule 23 (d).

The meaning of the Rule is quite clear. As at Wormhout, Dietrich's responsibility for the behaviour of the men under his command at Malmedy was without doubt.

For his part in the massacres at Malmedy, he was sentenced to 25 years' imprisonment. Unfortunately, in obtaining statements from SS-officers, interrogators treated their prisoners with brutality, thus placing themselves under the same condemnation as the accused Germans. This led to questions in the US Senate, particularly from Senator McCarthy – with the result that death sentences were commuted and terms of imprisonment reduced. Dietrich benefited by serving only 10 years of his sentence. His freedom was short-lived, for he was arrested and taken to Munich for trial in connection with the 30th June 1934 executions, known as the Röhm Purge. On 14th May 1957, he was sentenced to 18 months' imprisonment, and died shortly after his release.

CHAPTER FIFTEEN

To Be Believed

Halfway along the road from Wormhout to Esquelbecq is a Memorial which was erected in memory of those who died in and around the barn. The enclosure where the Memorial stands was presented by Monsieur Paul Marie de la Gorce, of Paris, as the result of correspondence between the author and the Mayor of Esquelbecq. The site was selected as being the nearest accessible spot to the site of the barn, which was demolished some time after 1947 and replaced by the one which stands near the situation of the original. Also, being situated at the side of the road, its inscription is clearly visible to travellers.

The ditch were Dietrich lay for several uncomfortable hours on the morning of the massacre, is no more than 25 yards away from the enclosure.

As the Commonwealth War Graves Commission was not disposed to carry out the work, the Memorial was made by Monsieur Naels, the Cassel stonemason, at cost. The money was provided mostly by members of the Dunkirk Veterans' Association as the result of an appeal by the Birmingham Branch, to which most of the survivors belong.

It was dedicated by the author on 28th May 1973, the anniversary of the massacre, and exactly a year after the author heard its story from Bill and Douglas Cordrey. Over two thousand people were present, including the Mayor of Esquelbecq and many local citizens. The British contingent consisted of members of branches of the DVA from all over the world, who were already in France for the Annual Pilgrimage to Dunkirk.

At that time, only four survivors had been traced: Daley, Evans,

Lavelle and Tombs, and these men unveiled the Memorial.

Immediately following the dedication of the Memorial, there was a Service which the author was privileged to conduct in the British Military Cemetery at Esquelbecq.

At last, there was a fitting Memorial to the memory of the men who were massacred. So long as the stone remains, all who pass from Wormhout to Esquelbecq will be reminded of a group of men who died after participating in a rearguard action which played its part in the evacuation of a whole army.

The inscription on the stone, reads:

To the Glory of God
and in memory
of the men
of
The Royal Warwickshire Regiment
The Cheshire Regiment
and
The Royal Artillery
who, on May 28th, 1940, were massacred
in a barn near this spot
also of the
men who were murdered as they were
being marched to the barn
'We will remember them'

The four men discovered in time for the unveiling of the Memorial were followed by Reginald West and George Hall, each of whom was interviewed by the author for the first time in 1973. Corporal Gill's last known address was in Middlesborough, and due to the efforts of Radio Teesside, the author was informed that he had died in 1972.

The tracing of Richard Parry proved difficult. One source of information said that he was in Yorkshire, which he was not: and an equally unreliable informant said that he was dead. Initial enquiries in Wales drew a blank, until a letter from the author to the Vicar of Llandudno revealed that old friends of Parrys were living in the town. They were able to supply his address.

George Hopper was the last to make himself known, until in 1976 the author discovered Jim Dutton, who was homeless.

If there are one or two other survivors alive, they have somehow failed to see the considerable amount of publicity which National and local newspapers have given to the dedication of the Memorial and the further annual visits made to the Cemetery. One man who was described to the author as being a survivor of the massacre, declined to offer information without monetary reward!

An experience common to each survivor was that people tended to disbelieve the story of the massacre. There is the man who, on telling his brother what had happened, was treated with frank scepticism, with the result that the two men have not spoken to each other since. Another survivor had not even told the story to his wife. When Reginald West gave details to a famous RAF officer who was interned with him in St Hippolyte, he laughed in West's face. This led to many of the men keeping the secret locked in their hearts.

What of the survivors, now?

Bert Evans lives in Northfield, Birmingham, and is employed as a Swimming Baths attendant, in Bournville. John Lavelle lives and works in Kidderminster. Charles Daley and George Hopper live in London. Richard Parry has retired from his veterinary practice, and lives on the shore of Lake Windermere. Reginald West and George Hall are both retired, and live in Great Barr and Cradley Heath, respectively. Alf Tombs still lives in Hall Green, Birmingham. Jim Dutton lives in Wolverhampton.

This means that nine men who suffered the agonies of the barn, are known to be alive.

Bill Cordrey lives and works in Somerset. George Merry, who witnessed some of the events in the Meadow, lives in Nuneaton. Colonel L. T. Tomes, whose private diary yielded much valuable information, lives at Hawkchurch, Axminster, Devon.

Most of the survivors bear the marks of their experiences on their bodies. All will never erase the memory from their minds. Charles Daley wears an artificial leg, and bears other scars. Bert Evans has one arm, and is marked by bullet and shrapnel wounds. Alf Tombs still has considerable trouble with the injury to his shin, which has never completely healed, and is in frequent pain. John Lavelle, likewise, has constant pain in his foot and suffers with his heart. The cheerful face of Richard Parry is marked by the bullet wound, and his legs are scarred.

For many years, most of the men suffered frequent and recurring nightmares in which the scenes in the barn figured vividly, as many of the wives testify. Yet none complain . . .

Several felt that they had been forgotten, and every one has wondered why so little has been said and written about what was one of the most harrowing stories of the Battle of France, 1940 – and not because they wanted to see it in print, but be believed.

In the case of every man who receives a disability pension, the amount awarded (as in respect of all war pensions) is derisory. For too long, the British people have been too easily content with the monetary insults which are handed out to men and women who suffer as the result of their contribution to the existence of a free society.

Two or three of the men are compelled to work in jobs which they would not choose, if they had not been disabled. One man who figures in the story was fêted by the Mayor of his town when he returned home – but no employer in the district has offered him a job when he has been out of work. At the time of writing, he earns his living brewing tea and fetching and carrying in a foundry for better rewarded men.

Another man is crippled, as is evident from his limp. Yet, some time ago, it was considered expedient for his pension to be withdrawn. After an appeal to his Member of Parliament, an allowance of just over £2 a week was granted. Explaining how he came to lose his pension, he said, 'I had to go for a medical check-up. The woman doctor asked if I lost time at work, and I had to say, "no".' Continuing, he said, 'You know, Padre, every day when I get up, I say to myself, "Can I make it to work?", and I feel the pain and think that I can't, but I drag myself along. And when I told the doctor that I didn't lose time at work, she said something about my disability not being as bad as all that . . .'

Whether the pension was curtailed as the result of medical 'opinion', it is not possible to say. But his pension was stopped.

That a man who came so close to giving his life 'for his friends' – of whom the well-paid doctor was one – should be so callously treated, is disgraceful.

To the credit of the Ministry of Social Security, the author's letter to their head office explaining the man's part in the massacre and his need, resulted in a vastly improved, and more worthy pension.

Another man's housing needs have been treated with cavalier indifference by officials of the Housing Department of the City where he lives, and it has been necessary for one to intervene on his behalf. The latest survivor to be traced has no fixed abode, and efforts are being made by the author to house him permanently.[1]

So, when the nine survivors and another man who features in the story were discovered, several were in need of help. From this, it is safe to assume that there must be a large number of men and women who, having served the nation at cost to themselves, have needs which are in danger of being overlooked. This, despite the excellent work of ex-service organisations which exist to serve such needs. But there are those who are reluctant to appeal to voluntary organisations because they feel that there are others, with prior needs.

There ought to be a Government Minister whose sole function should be to serve the interests of ex-Service men and women, and to whom they could feel able to turn, as of right. It is regrettable that men and women should be persuaded to join the Forces of the Crown in peacetime, and be conscripted in time of war, but left to the winds of chance. when they return to their homes.

None of the survivors of the Wormhout Massacre harbours any feelings of hatred, or resentment, in respect of the Germans. Despite the cruel manner in which they were treated by their captors, they have come to accept their sufferings as one of the misfortunes of war.

They and their murdered comrades deserve at least, that the story should be told . . .

[1] During the reading of the proofs for this book, a municipal flat was obtained for Jim Dutton, and Councillor J. Geraghty who assisted in this was by coincidence in 'D' Company at Wormhout, but escaped the massacre. The Wolverhampton Branch, DVA have also helped.

POSTSCRIPT TO SECOND EDITION, 1988

'The important thing is the search
and the process of enquiry, but
the process must be followed
with an alert understanding of
where we've got to from where.'

— Professor Myles Burnyeat

ONE

Where We've Got To

Incontrovertible Facts:
- A massacre of British soldiers, all unarmed prisoners-of-war, was perpetrated by members of the Waffen-SS in the vicinity of Wormhout, France, on 28th May 1940.
- The graves of the murdered men are in the adjacent area.
- Survivors of the atrocity lived to tell the story.
- The *Leibstandarte*-SS Adolf Hitler Regiment's First and Second Battalions were involved in the battle.
- Men of the Second Battalion performed the atrocity.
- The Commanding Officer of the LSSAH Regiment was Josef 'Sepp' Dietrich.
- The atrocity was not investigated by the German military authorities.
- Until the British survivors were repatriated from prisoner-of-war camps in 1943, the British authorities were unaware of the incident.

The Investigation:
- In March 1943, the Treasury Solicitor contacted six of the known survivors for the purpose of obtaining statements.
- Subsequently, a unit of the British War Crimes Interrogation Department, led by Lt Col A. P. Scotland, OBE, investigated the crime.
- Eleven German prisoners were identified as possible witnesses and held for questioning.
- Three British survivors were requested to present themselves at the 'London Cage', in Kensington, on 22nd April 1947, for the purpose of identifying Germans suspected as having taken part in the massacre.
- Identification proved negative.

155

- Three British survivors and one British witness were taken to Wormhout for the purpose of reconstructing the various locations and positions in the area of the French town.
- A preliminary report was sent to the Judge Advocate General.
- Colonel Scotland issued the final report to the JAG in June 1947.

TWO

In the Public Arena

James Spedding commented that every historian who is faced with a statement of fact, must ask the question: 'Who first said so, and what opportunities had he of knowing it?'.

Lt Colonel Scotland had the opportunity of knowing about the Wormhout massacre. He had received from the Judge Advocate General's Office statements made by a few British survivors of the massacre before a Commissioner for Oaths in the Treasury Solicitor's Office. Scotland and his staff had obtained statements from the Waffen-SS men who had been interrogated whilst in custody. Other statements had been made by a few inhabitants who lived in and around Wormhout: some of these were to the effect that wine had been stolen on the day of the atrocity by men of the *Leibstandarte*-SS Adolf Hitler Regiment. Scotland had the evidence of the murdered men's graves. He was the first person to place the story in the public arena, in his book *The London Cage*.

In the book, Scotland told the stories of several war crimes committed during the Second World War and which went unpunished: but of the Wormhout massacre he stated that no other case had filled him with a deeper sense of frustration. After relating the facts he lamented that despite his lengthy and painstaking investigations he had failed to 'obtain anything of value that might lead to identification of the guilty party. In short, I had no case to send to the Court.'.

However, he added that Wilhelm Mohnke, who was unavailable at the time 'was the man who could have assisted us, as the police say, in our enquiries.'.

One may feel some sympathy for Scotland, who first said so and had good opportunity of knowing it: but a wanted man is presumed to be innocent until his guilt can be established in court. It is fortunate that justice does not depend upon opinions which are expressed outside a court.

Elsewhere in *The London Cage,* Scotland writes of some atrocities which were committed soon after the D-Day landings. 'This time,' he states, 'it was not the British but the Canadian forces who came up against Nazi ruthlessness. At that time, the Germans responsible were not the low-grade elements of Totenkopf Regiments but the Hitler Youth Division, in which an important pair of leading Nazi lights were General Kurt Meyer, the Commander, and Major-General Mohnke, who commanded one of its Regiments. Both these men had been officers in the SS-*Leibstandarte* — Hitler's bodyguard — when the war began.'

In this context, Scotland related the first of what he called 'a string of murders' which took place in the Caen area, where bitter fighting occurred. It was during the first day's engagement between the Hitler Youth Forces and the Canadian troops on 7th June 1944 that three Canadians were unfortunate to be taken prisoner, early in the morning, and shot.

Scotland wrote that before the atrocity took place Wilhelm Mohnke, who could speak English, interrogated the prisoners himself.

However, in *The Trial of Kurt Meyer,* B. J. F. MacDonald asserts that the interrogation was conducted through an interpreter, in the presence of a German adjutant.

In Scotland's version of the shootings, the three Canadians were marched for a short distance until they reached a shell hole and were escorted by three German Regimental Field Policemen. On the edge of the cavity the men were shot, with their bodies falling into the crater. Two days later, some of the advancing Canadian troops discovered the bodies of their murdered comrades.

MacDonald's account differs . . .

He tells of a young Polish SS-conscript, referred to as 'W.S.', who was captured and taken to a prison camp in England. There, he related the story of the shootings: and over a year after the atrocity was perpetrated he was taken to the area. Instantly, he pointed out the positions where the German and Canadian soldiers had stood: and although the shell hole was filled with water to a depth of eight feet, it was located by 'W.S.' as the place where the bodies had fallen. The

Pole was even able to shew where the missing papers and other possessions which had been taken from the Canadian soldiers had been thrown, and these were recovered.

Divers managed to locate the bodies and the water was pumped out of the cavity. When the bodies were recovered, they were identified. It was established that the three men had died of multiple bullet holes.

'This,' wrote MacDonald, 'is typical of the thoroughness of our investigations.'

MacDonald went on: 'In due course, we filed with the United Nations War Crimes Commission in London our reports concerning the offences attributed to the 25th and 26th SS-Panzer Regiments and their respective Commanders. The Commission, headed by Lord Wright . . . found that prima facie cases had been established.'

At the end of the War, MacDonald was informed that Wilhelm Mohnke was supposed to be in a Russian prison camp: but the Russians, described by MacDonald as 'our intransigent Allies', had mislaid the file, or not heard from Moscow. In other words, they would not confirm or deny that Mohnke was being held by them. Nevertheless, as the Canadians were eager to interrogate Wilhelm Mohnke, in 1945 they sent an officer to the Russian HQ in Berlin with strict orders to sit there until he received a satisfactory answer. After three days, the Russians threatened to throw him out.

The only confirmation of Mohnke's whereabouts was received by MacDonald in a report from Major-General Schrieber, Surgeon-General of the German Army, that he had seen Mohnke in a prison camp at Strausberg, where Schrieber was interned.

'So,' MacDonald complained, 'we had to give up our efforts at this time.' But he had the satisfaction of knowing that his report concerning General Kurt Meyer resulted in his being sentenced by the Allied War Crimes Commission for his various offences, being released after four years in prison.

The above extracts from the writings of Scotland and MacDonald are reproduced merely to demonstrate that much care is needed in reading what has been placed in the public arena. The differences which are apparent in the two accounts lead one to question other evidence which may be presented. It follows that whichever investigator was incorrect, care is needed in assessing other material which he produced.

THREE

Mohnke, Alive!

Bert Evans was the first survivor of the massacre I traced and interviewed, in the summer of 1972. Nobody, not even his brother, had believed his story of the massacre and I promised him that I would write a book about his experiences, so that he would be believed. It was not until three years later that I discovered Jim Dutton, who was not on the list of survivors. Indeed, all my contacts had stated that he had died in the barn, or shortly afterwards.

When I visited Jim Dutton he was living in the bleak, windowless room of an empty house. Later, he was given the key of a flat and I visited him again.

'Padre,' he said, 'I thank God I'm settled, at last — but I can't get the barn out of my mind. I seek no revenge, but I do wish that justice could be done.'

I remembered that Bert Evans had uttered the same words when I first interviewed him: so I decided to take up the matter with the authorities from the point where Douglas Cordrey (from whom I first heard of the massacre in May 1972) had run into what appeared to be a bureaucratic fog. In an effort to obtain more information concerning the events of May 1940, he had written to the late Airey Neave, DSO, MC, MP.

Airey Neave replied, enclosing a letter from the Secretary of State for the Army, Mr Peter Blaker, MP. The letter stated that the Cabinet Office could not help and that none of the documents which were held could reveal closer figures than 80 to 90, as these concerned the men who were massacred.

'I am sorry,' the letter went on, 'to say that I can offer no useful information on Wilhelm Mohnke. As you know, the task of tracing and investigating Nazi War Crimes was handed over to the German authorities at the beginning of 1950, when the Central Office for the Prosecution of National Socialist War Crimes was set up. It may be, therefore, that the German authorities can now best advise Mr Cordrey on this aspect of his research. I am sorry I cannot be more helpful.'

I decided to contact Sir Donald Kaberry, Bt, MP, who was the legal adviser to the Dunkirk Veterans' Association. He wrote to the Ministry of Defence and received a reply, part of which read: 'Our previous attempts to unearth information for Mr Cordrey through the Judge Advocate General's Office, the Cabinet Office and other sources have unfortunately been unsuccessful and I very much regret therefore that I am unable to help. Mr Aitken has now written direct to this Ministry about copyright aspects of material he has sighted and wishes to use, and he should by now have received our reply.'

So, two prominent Members of Parliament were unable to throw any more light on the subject than was already known to Douglas Cordrey and me. I asked myself whether the Government knew more than it was prepared to vouchsafe to Mr Airey Neave and Sir Donald Kaberry for my benefit. Apparently the Government knew nothing of the whereabouts of Wilhelm Mohnke who was assumed by most historians to be in East Germany, where he was more likely to settle after release from Russian custody. As a man wanted by the Canadians he was unlikely to settle in West Germany. Indeed, there were those who thought that Mohnke was dead.

Then, by an amazing coincidence, I attended a dinner at which a number of German ex-soldiers were the guests. After the meal I found myself in conversation with a retired, high-ranking German officer of the Wehrmacht. I asked him if he had known 'Sepp' Dietrich.

'Yes,' he replied, 'He was a remarkable man.'

'Did you ever meet Wilhelm Mohnke?', I asked.

'I have only heard stories,' he said, 'but that is all.'

'I have heard and read,' I went on, 'that he is in East Germany, or even dead.'

'Yes, that would be so,' he commented, 'and I have heard that he is alive, and living in Lübeck — but that is quiet gossip!'

I was intrigued: and on 29th August 1973 I wrote to the Ludwigsburg office of the department for the Prosecution of National Socialist War

Crimes. In my letter I informed them that I was currently engaged in writing a book whose purpose was to relate the massacre of British unarmed prisoners of war at Wormhout, in 1940. I named the 2nd Battalion of the LSSAH as the unit from which members had been selected to act as executioners. I stated that an investigation had been held by the British authorities, with survivors and German soldiers giving statements: and I added that as Brigadeführer Wilhelm Mohnke was not available for questioning at the time he was listed with the UNO. I asked whether, if Mohnke was alive, it was possible for him to be questioned in relation to his alleged complicity.

On 14 November 1973 I received a courteous reply in which friendly greetings were expressed. The letter gave a brief account of Mohnke's career from 28 June 1933 until the time of his appointment as Commander of Hitler's bunker. The letter stated that my submissions would receive attention.

Here, I should say that before writing to Ludwigsburg I consulted a friend who was a highly qualified lawyer with a judicial appointment. I supplied him with all the documents in my possession and requested his opinion of the case as it stood in 1947. After a couple of weeks he told me that, in his opinion and based upon the information I had given him, there was no positive evidence that Wilhelm Mohnke either knew of, or had condoned the atrocity at Wormhout. He did, however, feel inclined to think that there was a slightly better case to answer regarding the murder of Canadian soldiers in 1944.

I next received a letter from Germany, dated 18 January 1974. Addressed from Lübeck, it was signed WIRSICH (State Prosecutor). After the usual greetings, it read:

Subject:
Investigations into the affair of SS-Brigadeführer and Generalmajor of the Waffen-SS, Wilhelm Mohnke . . . (my dots replace the address, at a village near Hamburg), suspected of having committed War Crimes.
Ref:
Your letter of the 29.8.73 addressed to the Central Office of the Administration of Justice, Ludwigsburg.

Your letter has been passed to me by the Central Office. You state that the (Businessman) Wilhelm Mohnke, who was Führer in the 11th Batt of the SS-Panzer Division *Leibstandarte* Adolf Hitler, took part in the unlawful shooting of 90 soldiers of the Royal Warwickshire Regiment on the 28 May 1940 in Wormhout, France.

According to statements in Dr Klietmann's book, *The Waffen-SS,* a document published by Der Freiwilligen, it states:

The SS-Panzer Division Adolf Hitler at the time in question was called the *Leibstandarte*-SS Adolf Hitler and took part in the attack on Dunkirk and in particular in the assault on Wormhout. There was also a 2nd Battalion to which the 5 Company belonged but there is no evidence that this section took part in the shooting of 90 soldiers of the Warwickshire Regiment. It is possible that at this time Mohnke, Führer of the 5 Co, was there. As far as is known he was attached to the Waffen-SS from 1933 until the end of the War. From 21.6.1943 he was attached to the *Leibstandarte*-SS Adolf Hitler, after which he was in command of the 2 Panzer Grenadier Regiment (12) to which the SS-Panzer Grenadier was attached, having previously been the 1 SS Panzer Division *Leibstandarte* Adolf Hitler. From about June 1944 to 6 February 1945, Mohnke was again transferred to the 1 SS Panzer Division *Leibstandarte* Adolf Hitler as their Commander.

Your description of Mohnke as a suspected War criminal has not been proved. I can see no possibility of this complex question being further explained. If you can give further information I shall be grateful.

I have therefore filed this matter.

WIRSICH (State Lawyer)

I read the letter with amazement, for with the exception of the important information that Mohnke was alive and living at an address which had been kindly supplied to me, there was information only from the notable Dr Klietmann which, if correctly quoted, was hardly well researched. It seemed that Dr Klietmann was not aware that just before the massacre Mohnke had been promoted from Commander of 5 Company to the position of Battalion Commanding Officer. I was astounded that the

State lawyer's best information was from such a source, even though from the hand of Dr Klietmann.

My reply read:

Dear Herr Wirsich,
Thank you for your letter.

First, may I say that my letter addressed to Ludwigsburg was in connection with a book I hope to write concerning the massacre by the German SS of between 60 and 90 British soldiers at Wormhout, France, on 28th May 1940. One purpose in writing to Ludwigsburg was, if possible, to obtain more information than I already possess regarding the crime in general and Major-General Mohnke in particular.

Information previously available to me suggested that he was either in the Eastern zone of Germany, or dead. However, from your kind reply I gather that he is alive and living at the address which you give. This will, if you can confirm it, enable me to say in the book that Mohnke is alive: but, of course, I shall not publish his whereabouts.

It appears from the information which you kindly give me that I have more knowledge of Mohnke's alleged complicity in the murder of British and Canadian soldiers than you possess. For your information, I enclose copies of material from (a) a book written by Colonel Scotland, the British investigator for the War Crimes unit. The book is entitled: *The London Cage.* (b) A book written about the trial of Kurt Meyer, called *The Trial of Kurt Meyer.* This mentions the alleged complicity of Major-General Mohnke. You will also see from the enclosures, that Colonel Scotland was not able to trace Mohnke in order to interrogate him for his alleged part in the massacre at Wormhout. You will notice that he says: 'There was little doubt in my mind that not only Moenke (Mohnke) knew what had happened at Paradis (a place near to Wormhout and where, the day previously, 98 men were massacred by another German unit), but was himself not averse to the elimination of prisoners.' You will also see that if there is a certain amount of doubt regarding Mohnke's complicity at Wormhout, there is less doubt about his alleged part in murders of prisoners in 1944.

I write not from any official standing, but as National Chaplain of the Dunkirk Veterans' Association. It is because members of the Association who are known to me were survivors of the Wormhout massacre that I wish to write about it — not in a spirit of revenge, but to place on record the experiences of some brave men in the face of great peril and danger.

In giving you the additional information you require, I leave it with you to decide how to proceed with the matter. You may feel it right, in the interests of the good name of Germany, to make investigations of your own, based upon the initial information I have supplied.

Yours sincerely,

LESLIE AITKEN

I received a reply, dated 21st February 1974, requesting details of the books listed, their authors and publishers. These were supplied. There was a long silence, broken when I received a letter from Wirsich, dated 18th February 1976. By that time my book had been cleared by the Ministry of Defence and published — which accounts for the revelation concerning Mohnke's availability not being mentioned in the first edition of the book.

The letter read:

Subject:

Preliminary investigations against the Major-General Wilhelm Mohnke on account of War Crimes.

Ref:

Your last letter, dated 6.3.1974.

Dear Mr Aitken,

On the basis of your several informations extensive investigations have been instituted. The accused Mohnke has denied the deed, reproached in the books of Scotland and MacDonald. The interrogation of all former still to ascertain members of the SS-tank Division 'Hitlerjugend' have brought no essential facts to the crimes in question. The author of the book *London Cage* is deceased. MacDonald could not be ascertained in Canada. Should it not be possible for you to name persons who can make statements to the events in question, I have to discontinue the proceedings, because the existing means of proof are not enough.

Yours respectfully,

WIRSICH

I remained determined and repeated the facts in my reply: and the response came from the State Attorney. Dated 15th June 1976, it read:

Subject:

Investigations procedure against Generals Meyer, Wilhelm Mohnke, concerning War Crimes.

Reference

Documents from 18 January 1974 and further correspondence.

Dear Mr Aitken,

After thorough investigation, accusations of War Crimes by the accused Mohnke were not sufficient to indict him of the facts of the case of which he is accused in the books of Scotland and MacDonald. It is not impossible that the mentioned War Crimes from Commanders of other units have taken place. Concerning Commander Meyer of the 25 Regiment, and Commander Siebken of the 2nd Regiment, both were made responsible for War Crimes by the Allied War Crimes Tribunal. Siebken was executed in 1948 and Meyer is now dead.

In view of the above information, further investigation is useless.

Respectfully yours,

BÖTTCHER

It was obvious to me that the end of the matter as this concerned the German Authorities had been reached, but it was not the end of the road, for there was one card left for me to play. I wrote a letter at considerable length to the Canadian authorities, stating all the facts as presented to Ludwigsburg and Lübeck. I knew the Canadians had been very anxious to settle the matter which had been pending since 1946 due to Mohnke's unavailability. Now that he was known to be alive and living in West Germany I felt sure that the Canadians would push hard at this particular door.

They replied saying that they had found my letter very interesting and certain steps would be taken. The letter concluded: 'I trust that this action will prove helpful.'

After over two years, the result was leaked to me unofficially, in a signed letter. Part of it read:

Of course, the investigation arising from your information increased my interest. I was able to confirm your statements in detail. In the weeks 8th-14th June, 1944, Mohnke's name was connected with six incidents in Normandy involving the murder of at least 59 Canadian soldiers. A charge sheet was prepared on the basis of four of them, and our legal officers were prepared to prosecute him if he could be found. Unfortunately, the key witness, the one who could positively identify him and connect him with the murders, was a Polish SS man who was repatriated by an administrative error before his interrogation was completed or all hope of finding Mohnke was abandoned.

This, of course, was already known to me, but I was interested in the next paragraph:

It is now almost two years since I handed in my report, and I know that it was forwarded to the appropriate authorities for action. Consequently, I assume that no action can be taken now for lack of witnesses.

It was the end of the road: but I had done my best for the survivors of the Wormhout massacre. However, as in 1947, the situation after lengthy enquiries had been made, with questions asked, was that there is no case to present in Court. The evidence today is no more conclusive than it was after Scotland presented his report. Indeed, with the passing of time many witnesses have died. Unless and until the case comes to court, Wilhelm Mohnke's alleged guilt cannot be established.

Since my correspondence with the German authorities, Jim Dutton has died, as have Richard Parry, John Lavelle and George Hall . . .

FOUR

Questions in the House

For a number of years Reginald West, one of the massacre survivors, had been in regular contact with his member of Parliament, Mr Jeff Rooker, concerning some difficulties with a Prisoner of War Fund which is administered by Trustees on behalf of the Royal Warwickshire Regimental Association. Mr Rooker is indefatigable in the service of his constituents and when he heard that Reginald West was ill, he visited him at his home early in 1988.

During the conversation Reginald West mentioned that he was troubled because the men responsible for the massacre at Wormhout had not been brought to trial: and Mr Rooker resolved to raise the matter in the House of Commons. So, on 21st April 1988, Jeff Rooker asked the Home Secretary, Mr Douglas Hurd, whether he would 'bring to account the former Nazi officer, Wilhelm Mohnke, of Hamburg. The massacre of over 80 unarmed members of the Royal Warwickshire Regiment which happened in 1940, happened as though it was yesterday for survivors like my constituent, 81-year-old Reg West. Mr West and other survivors are still seeking justice for themselves and their fallen comrades. We owe it to them.'.

The Home Secretary replied, saying that the relevant material at the Defence Ministry was being 'rigorously re-examined to see if there is information which can provide the basis for the kind of action you are proposing'. He told a Tory questioner that Sir Geoffrey Howe, Foreign Secretary, and George Younger, Secretary for Defence, would 'consider in the light of the examination whether any representations should be made to the Government of the Federal Republic of Germany'. He also made it clear that Mohnke was outside the jurisdiction of the British courts and that there was little prospect of seeking his extradition.

During the following weekend the Press continued to be active. What were variously purported to be revelations were exclusively divulged. It was stated in *The Sunday Times* that shortly after Mr Rooker raised the matter in the House of Commons he was handed a copy of what was described as 'a secret file'. Readers were informed that the 'file' had been passed to *The Sunday Times;* and details which were not for public consumption were revealed in heavy, black print. Readers were solemnly informed that the information which had been spelt out as being examined by senior ministers was 'under strict Government embargo until the year 2022'. (In fact, the reports are closed, under the Official Secrets Act, until 1st January 2021.) It was further stated that 'the 72-page, 20,000 word report, compiled by the British War Crimes Interrogation unit in 1947, names . . . the officer who ordered the killings of unarmed soldiers captured near the French village of Wormhout, close to Dunkirk'.

'Included in the file,' the report continued, 'are the names of other SS-men — some still living in West Germany — who played key roles in the killings in May, 1940, of men from the Royal Warwickshire and Cheshire Regiments and the Royal Artillery . . . the material being studied by Whitehall officials makes grim reading and presents them with a legal and diplomatic minefield. Faced with their own evidence . . . the Government will be pushed to act, or stand accused of "protecting a war criminal".'

There followed a statement which had been offered by a Mr Anthony Terry, who gave it as his opinion that 'There's always been a reluctance on the part of Whitehall to pursue these people. I don't know what the reasons were, but I discovered later there were political reasons why they didn't want to pursue Nazis at that time. We certainly did our best to collect the material, but we were hamstrung in London.'

Wilhelm Mohnke was quoted as having stated to a German reporter: 'I have never concealed a thing, unlike Waldheim. I was in Dunkirk. It's true. But what kind of beasts must they have been to slaughter prisoners of war with bayonets and so on? This is an appalling crime.'

The Sunday Times article was excellent journalism, especially when compared with the 'Nazi With Two Glass Eyes' type of headline which appeared elsewhere in the Press at that time. However, what *The Sunday*

Times could not know was that the 'secret file' with which they had been presented was redundant, having been superseded by another.

Two weeks later, when the publicity had died down, I received a telephone call from a German journalist, Dr M. MacDonald, whose father was a Scot. He stated that he had interviewed Wilhelm Mohnke at considerable length. 'He was absolutely overpowering,' he remarked, 'and he is admired by many of the people in the district where he resides. Indeed, some of them regard him as a kind of guru.'

During the Press coverage of the events following the question in the House of Commons it emerged that Mr Brian Fahey, of Strathclyde, was a survivor of the massacre. An ex-Artillery soldier, it seems that his experiences at Wormhout were not known to the War Crimes Interrogation Unit.

FIVE

The Secret Whitehall File

The existence of the War Crimes Interrogation Unit's report was known to me in 1972. It is a lengthy document and not a file, as it has been called in the Press: for an office file is a device which enables documents to be kept in order. Lest it be thought that one is being tautological, this is not the intention, for to differentiate between the terms is helpful in reaching an opinion as to the nature of the 'secret file'.

The reference number ascribed to the leaked report of the War Crimes Interrogation Unit was revealed to me by *The Sunday Times,* but it will be described here as 'WR(Wormhout Report)/123/456'. However, what *The Sunday Times* could not have known at the time their article appeared is that the document bearing the reference number 'WR/123/456' was superseded by another. To this, one will give the reference 'WR/123/457'. It follows that the document under the reference number 'WR/123/456' and which aroused such curiosity, is not the final report. Presumably the two documents are kept together in the 'secret file'.

An important question is: are there other documents in this file? One wonders if the person who illegally leaked document 'WR/123/456' was aware that he presented *The Sunday Times* with a 'pig in a poke'. He seems to have been in a position, at some time, to have seen the first report. How he has been allowed to retain it is another question. However close he may have been to the enquiries made in 1947, it is extremely unlikely that he has had access to the 'secret file' which is said to be held in Whitehall.

So far as the two reports are concerned, their confidentiality is so classified because their release for scrutiny by the general public could be sensitive to persons who are mentioned in each report, that is, German witnesses and British survivors. The words on the front cover of each report, CONFIDENTIAL: CROWN COPYRIGHT, were not printed because some Government official derived satisfaction in being miserly with the general public. Rather was it that innocent persons should be protected from opinions reached as the result of a hasty reading of the reports, for care has to be exercised when reading such documents. Indeed, the reports contain glaring factual inaccuracies which are surprising in documents of such importance: and these would be misleading to one who has not had the advantage of researching every aspect of the topic at considerable length.

That there has been no 'cover-up' concerning Wilhelm Mohnke's link, whatever that may have been, with the atrocity is known to me. One of the few provisos which were made to me by the Ministry of Defence when I was originally writing my book was that I should avoid naming German soldiers in a certain context — 'apart from Wilhelm Mohnke, who has received fairly wide publicity'. This, of course, was not an invitation for me to defame him by uttering allegations which could not be proved.

When I sought permission to quote from various sources this was freely given by the Ministry of Defence, who assumed that I had seen the Wormhout report: and I was allowed to make use of it, provided I made no reference to its existence. This, I consider, was both generous and fair. Every stage in the original production of the manuscript was presented to the Ministry of Defence and approved. The final manuscript received approval, together with the remark: 'Our Historical Branch read the MSS with interest and commented that the first hand accounts which you have used give the manuscript a quality of immediacy which made the text easy to read.' The Judge Advocate General's Office gladly consented to my use in the book of the survivors' affidavits; and the published book was sent to the Ministry of Defence for inclusion in their archives.

I relate the above account of my correspondence with the Ministry of Defence and the Judge Advocate General's Office, which occupied a period of three years, so as to shew the reasons for its classification as confidential. If the Wormhout report contained awful State or political secrets I would not have been given permission to use it, even if employed in a responsible manner. It is essential to realize that the Wormhout report is a document which gives an outline of troops' dispositions, an account of the battle, statements by German witnesses and British survivors, together with a conclusion. To the non-specialist reader looking for exciting revelations it would merely produce a yawn, although it provides interesting reading for a military historian.

Could there be documents other than 'WR/123/456' and 'WR/123/457' reposing securely in the 'Secret Whitehall File'? If so, for what reason? Is it that someone mentioned in other documents in, or cross-referenced with, the file is politically interesting on account of what he knew, or still knows? Apart from 'Sepp' Dietrich, the most interesting person mentioned in the Wormhout report(s) is Wilhelm Mohnke. Dietrich was a swashbuckling type of Nazi General who was liked by his men, but he is not politically intriguing to the curious. Also, if there are interesting political facts which are known relating to Wilhelm Mohnke they cannot be connected with Wormhout, or his involvement in other battle areas.

Some interesting information which relates to Wilhelm Mohnke is contained in *The Bormann Brotherhood,* written by William Stevenson. My notes on the information which concerns us are as follows . . .

A brief mention is made of Mohnke's being 'hunted' for alleged complicity in connection with the massacre of Canadian soldiers. It is also related that the Canadian Army wished to secure him for questioning, but were frustrated because he was in Russian hands (pp 97 and 207).

Details are given of Mohnke's escape from Hitler's bunker at the end of the 1939-45 War and his capture by the Russians. He is said to have helped the Russians to locate the remains of the bunker in Berlin, and was able to supply the names of important personnel who surrounded Hitler during his last days. The Russians took care to inform Mohnke that he was being sought by the Canadians for questioning and trial. So as to ensure that he would not be handed over to the vengeful Canadians, Mohnke is said to have informed the Russians of what he had seen and heard in the bunker: and it is alleged that what he did not know, he invented. He was also claimed to have given an account of alleged secret communications which took place between Nazi leaders and the West (pp 209 & 210).

On information supplied by captured men such as Mohnke, the

Russians were led to believe that part of the Nazi plan for survival was to persuade the Western Allies that Hitler had been foolhardy, not only on account of his management of the war, but in failing to realize that the real enemy was the Soviet Union. Moreover, the Allied Intelligence Services were aware that Mohnke was talking freely to his Russian captors; so, whenever the Canadians enquired about his availability, the Russians provided embarrassing accounts of what Mohnke was supposed to have said (p 212).

When the Canadians presented another firm request for news of Mohnke which might lead to his capture by them, the Russians merely stated that they had noted the appointment of 'Panzermeyer' (Kurt Meyer), who had been sentenced for War Crimes but released after four years for service with the NATO forces in Europe. The Russians added: 'These forces, as is well known, are directed against the democratic republics . . . Imperialist war-mongers have permitted Nazis to return to their former military and civic positions' (p 212).

The information in William Stevenson's book which relates to Wilhelm Mohnke is far more interesting than the details in the Wormhout report about his activities at Wormhout. The background detail accords with recorded history: for behind Hitler's back, Nazi leaders had connived so as to probe the possibilities of a deal with the Western Allies. All the information is now filed in Russian, British, American and Canadian archives: and what Wilhelm Mohnke knew and remembers is but fragmentary in comparison.

There are those who, on reading what William Stevenson records in his book without having studied the history of the period in detail, have concluded that Wilhelm Mohnke is in possession of State shattering secrets. Certainly he could tell interesting tales of the comings and goings in the bunker. His free talk with the Russians after capture makes interesting reading: but the most that can be said is that the wily Russians were using Mohnke as a small pawn in a devious political game.

SIX

Waffen-SS Apologists

In mid-November 1977, two ex-Colonels of the Waffen-SS arrived in London for the purpose of launching the English edition of a book *Wenn Alle Brüder Schweigen (When All the Brothers are Silent)*. It was published on behalf of the Association of the former Waffen-SS. Most of the book, which contains 600 pages, has photographs of members of the Waffen-SS as they were 'thirty years ago, and more'. They are seen in pastoral settings milking cows, playing musical instruments and saying goodbye to their families. They are shewn marching, manning their guns and resting after action.

The publicity which attended the visit of the two ex-Colonels provoked angry comment in the Press, some from people who had suffered at the hands of the SS. The debate was extended on radio and television: and I was invited by the BBC to speak in a programme on which SS-Obersturmführer Hubert Meyer, one of the ex-Colonels, was to appear. Reginald West, a survivor of the Wormhout massacre, accompanied me to Broadcasting House and Richard Parry, another survivor, was linked to the programme from a studio in Carlisle.

I was asked to introduce the subject of the Waffen-SS and speak of the formation and development of the *Leibstandarte*-SS Regiment. The interviewer then raised the subject of the atrocity in May 1940, adding that the two survivors wished to put questions to Hubert Meyer, who was described as having served with the LSSAH at Wormhout.

Hubert Meyer was asked by the interviewer if he remembered the battle.

'I remember,' he replied, 'that it was one place where heavy fighting took place. I did not know of a War Crime, at that time . . .'

'Colonel,' Reginald West interrupted, 'who gave the order that no prisoners were to be taken?'

'Nobody gave an order at this time that no prisoners should be taken,' was the reply.

'That's a lie!' West exclaimed.

'I didn't know that this happened,' Meyer said. 'But, you know, I think that at every time in World War Two, crimes in the front line happened on both sides.'

As Hubert Meyer was an adjutant in the *Leibstandarte*'s 3rd Battalion, he was telling the truth as this concerned his ignorance of the episode. The 3rd Battalion of the LSSAH Regiment did not participate in the battle at Wormhout, as it had been placed in reserve before Battalions 1 and 2 were ordered to make the attack. He is one Waffen-SS member amongst others who, so far as I am aware, was not personally involved in atrocities. From such evidence as I have, the 3rd Battalion appears to have had officers who did not tolerate bullies and brawlers. On the other hand, the 2nd Battalion appears to have been singularly involved in brutality.

From the list of alleged LSSAH atrocities which appears on a later page, it is apparent that the 2nd Battalion was involved in a series of atrocities in Poland — seven months before the Regiment arrived in Wormhout. Indeed, Wilhelm Mohnke assumed command of the Battalion only about an hour before the alleged order for the despatching of the British prisoners. Mohnke was said to have remarked when the German escort brought the prisoners to the Battalion Headquarters: 'What do you mean bringing in prisoners, contrary to orders?' If such orders had been given by Mohnke they could hardly have reached platoon level by that time. In any case, such orders must have been operative when the Battalion was in Poland, 28 weeks beforehand.

The crimes, which were perpetrated on four separate occasions and in different locations, must have been known to 'Sepp' Dietrich, the Regimental Commander of the LSSAH. One is led to wonder why he failed, after the incidents in Poland, to discipline the officers of the murderous collection of Nazis belonging to the 2nd Battalion. Further, it is on record in Scotland's *The London Cage* that when he was appraised of the events at Wormhout he invoked the SS-oath, merely so as to cover up the details of the massacre and prevent an enquiry at Divisional level. Hence, he failed to cleanse the 2nd Battalion of its criminal elements, because its members continued to live down to their collective reputation as an ill-disciplined assortment of bullies and psychopathic killers.

The LSSAH was claimed to be an elite Guard Regiment, but its Commander, 'Sepp' Dietrich, must bear the sole responsibility for the less laudatory facts concerning his unit and the men under his command. Undoubtedly, he was a brave Commander in battle: but in regard to the behaviour of his men in the 2nd Battalion, he was an extraordinarily lax one.

It is this contradiction between the military proficiency of the earlier SS-units, especially the LSSAH, and the deplorable behaviour of a hard core of bullies which causes some concern to Waffen-SS apologists. They are intent on demonstrating that the original units were well and professionally trained by such men as Paul Hausser and Felix Steiner. Some have a wistful admiration for the masculine exhibitionism of 'Sepp' Dietrich. They are proud that the Waffen-SS was engaged in the toughest areas of those battles which were the bloodiest in the war of 1939-45, described as 'where the real men were'. In battle they fought with distinction — but the apologists are presented with other facts which are disconcerting.

In his foreword to *Wenn Alle Brüder Schweigen,* Paul Hausser quoted a statement made by General Guderian: 'The soldiers of the Waffen-SS fought shoulder to shoulder with the regular soldiers and the longer the war went on, the more they counted as "some of ours".'

The anonymous author of the book begins with the claim that the Waffen-SS was created out of a new spirit of the time when, in the 1930s, the new formation attracted the attention of men who were liable for military service. Recruits were motivated by 'political convictions, idealism, the desire to change society, the opportunity for advancement, and simple-co-incidence . . . they paid due respect to the image which their fathers portrayed. They also accorded the older generation recognition for their war service and held them in high esteem. For this reason, the new concept of "soldiering" did not represent a break with tradition, nor were the spiritual prerequisites lacking — they were, in fact, already present. No counter movement aimed at offering resistance to the Army was either planned or organised'.

Recruits were attracted to the Waffen-SS, claims the writer: 'because the formation was conceived of as a guard, as an elite: and this was the way it appeared to itself. It was considered an honour to have served in a Guard Regiment, and the people honoured those who had done so with respect and acclamation'.

Denials are made in the book that members of the Waffen-SS were military enthusiasts who 'enjoyed war for the sake of war, or trained from the perspective of political philosophy. Those who make such allegations could not have stood "among the men".'.

The book has a section entitled 'Defeat', in which bitter complaint is made regarding the post-war treatment of Waffen-SS members, who 'even if they did not belong any longer to front line units but had been released from service as a result of war wounds before the end of the war, all of them, even those in hospitals, were brought to Allied Camps. Later, they were subjected to a political cleansing process before Courts — the de-Nazification process. After years of war service with all its sacrifices and hardships, these men, because of their membership of the Waffen-SS, were forced to pay fines, suffer loss of freedom often with forced labour, were limited in the profession which they could pursue and were sometimes prohibited from practising their trades: they were also excluded from benefits. If they had suffered serious war wounds, this could be looked upon as grounds for clemency. Their survivors, widows and orphans were not excluded from these measures. They were not provided with the benefits to which they were entitled.'.

The last section of the book begins with a German saying 'Where there is much light, there are also many shadows.' Applied to the Waffen-SS, the writer protests on behalf of its ex-members 'against the tendency to accentuate and overstate the darker side, while at the same time playing down and belittling the brighter side'.

The writer charges many historians and writers of a tendency to spare others from the spotlight which they have directed upon the Waffen-SS. He adds: 'a complete illumination would shew the actual state of affairs and would illustrate that in other places as well, there are to be found shadows as well as light'.

In conclusion, it is stated that fears were expressed after the war regarding the future behaviour of ex-Nazis: and it is submitted that: 'No veteran of the Waffen-SS has thrown a hand grenade in the post-war society'.

It is natural that ex-members of elite Waffen-SS units should feel proud of their military expertise. Nevertheless, the honour of their Regiments was stained by enormities perpetrated by their more fanatical comrades. These were not isolated incidents, such as are committed by both sides in most wars, for they manifest an undeniable pattern of consistency.

In the Weiner Library, London, there is a copy of a Nuremburg document which lists all the known crimes alleged to have been committed by Waffen-SS units, about 18 in all. The document contains 28 pages. Deeds which are so diabolical as to defy description are briefly listed on each page. Appropriately, the first two pages refer to known crimes which are alleged to have been perpetrated by the elite unit of the Waffen-SS: the *Leibstandarte*-SS Adolf Hitler Regiment. When it was formed, it was a Company (SS-Sturm) of 120 men. On 22nd October 1943, the unit obtained its final title: 1 SS Panzer Division *Leibstandarte* 'Adolf Hitler'. When the Division was transferred from the East to Italy, just short of 150 trains were required to move the unit — without its armour.

During its 12 years' existence the *Leibstandarte* had four Commanders: SS Obergruppenführer und General der Waffen-SS Josef ('Sepp') Dietrich
    17 March 1933 to 27 July 1943
SS Brigadeführer und Generalmajor der Waffen-SS Theodor Wisch
    27 July 1943 to 20 August 1944
SS Oberführer Wilhelm Mohnke
    20 August 1944 to 6 February 1945
SS Brigadeführer und Generalmajor der Waffen-SS Otto Kumm
    6 February 1945 to 8 May 1945

SEVEN

A Question of Responsibility

When these pages were being finalised, Christopher Jeans, an ATV producer, spent four hours with me discussing certain aspects relating to a programme which he hoped to televise concerning the massacre. In the following week a film unit went to Wormhout, with a few of the survivors. Locations were filmed and an outline of the barn (long since demolished) was constructed in timber framework. The survivors were interviewed and the story was told. Next, the TV unit visited the State Prosecutor in Lübeck and reminded him that a recent statement made by Reginald West had been sent to him. Another statement was handed over, together with a copy of *Massacre on the Road to Dunkirk*. The programme, during which I was interviewed, was televised as *The Cook Report,* on 7 June 1988.

It is understood that the Lübeck State Prosecutor has re-opened the case concerning Mohnke. As my evidence presented in 1973-76 was deemed inadmissible for lack of positive witnesses, it appears that the burden of accusation will rest upon personal responsibility. Whatever Mohnke's connection with the massacre, he was the CO of the 2nd Battalion LSSAH when the prisoners were assembled for disposal, of whatever kind. As 'Sepp' Dietrich said: 'The Commander is responsible for the actions and conduct of his Regiment.'

One is intrigued concerning Dietrich's part in the events of 28th May 1940. His recovery from the ditch in which he hid for *seven hours* was timed at 1700 hrs, which coincided with the time of the massacre: but the fighting had moved from the vicinity of the ditch long before that time. Indeed, it was considered safe for the execution squad to move into the barn area, which was not far from the ditch.

Was the time of Dietrich's recovery the subject of a generally agreed lie? If so, is it possible that he was present when the order for the disposal of the prisoners was given? Or, was it as a result of sheer coincidence that he was rescued at the approximate time of the massacre? In 1973, I shewed pictures of two SS officers to one survivor. He was able to recognize only one of the men, of whose name he was unaware, and he pointed to the photograph of 'Sepp' Dietrich . . .

APPENDICES

The Survivors' Statements to the Judge Advocate General's Office

Charles Edward Daly

I, Charles Edward Daly, formerly of the 2nd Battalion The Royal Warwickshire Regiment, (Army Number 7342734) and now discharged from the Army and resident at xxx make oath and say as follows:-

1. I enlisted in the Army on the 17th December 1930 and after completing seven years service, was placed on the Reserve in March 1938. On the 2nd September 1939 I was recalled to the Colours and posted to 'A' Company. Two weeks later I proceeded with the Battalion overseas.

2. Towards the end of May 1940, in the course of military operations consequent on the invasion by German troops of Belgium, the Battalion was in the neighbourhood of a place called Wormhoudt, and was in action for about two days in defence of that place, against a force of Germans who were attacking with overwhelming superiority. By the afternoon of the 27th or 28th May 1940 or thereabouts, although we had not yielded our positions we had been surrounded, and our ammunition having given out, we surrendered and were made prisoners of war. A German soldier armed with a revolver shouted at me "Englander schwein" and shot me in the shoulder.

3. My Commanding Officer, Major Chichester Constable, had been killed on the previous day, and the rest of the Company was almost wiped out. The remnants were made prisoners and were marched to where the remnants of 'D' Company, who had also been made prisoners, were assembled. Some interrogation took

place of prisoners of war, including myself by the Officer in charge of the party. I do not know his rank, but he had around the sleeve of his tunic, between the elbow and the wrist, to the best of my recollection and belief, two bands of silver braid, and between them the name 'Adolf Hitler'.

4.   From this point, with some other ranks of the Cheshire Regiment and the Royal Artillery, we were marched to a barn some distance away, rather more than a mile as I judged. According to my estimate there were about ninety altogether who were herded into the barn, more or less filling it. A German soldier at the door stooped to pick a hand-grenade from his jack boot. Captain Lynn-Allen who was Commanding 'D' Company and who was the only officer amongst the prisoners, protested against what appeared to be the intention, namely, to massacre the prisoners. He also protested that there were a number of wounded, and that the accommodation was insufficient to give them room to lie down. The German soldier shouted back, 'Yellow Englishman, there will be plenty of room where you're all going to.' This man spoke fluent English, with a strong American accent. He and others then threw bombs into the barn. Some of these bombs were smothered by the heroic action of Sergeant Moore and C.S.M. Jennings who threw themselves on them and were immediately killed. One bomb in the direction of Captain Lynn Allen appeared to wound a man of his Company called Evans, and I saw Captain Lynn Allen take advantage of the Germans taking cover from the explosion of the bombs, to drag Private Evans out of the barn, and try and make an escape. I did not see what happened to them after that, but I was subsequently informed and verily believe, that Capt. Lynn Allen was killed, and that Private Evans was shot and left for dead but recovered, and has since been repatriated.

5.   Following this throwing of bombs into the barn, the Germans began taking the prisoners of war out of the barn five at a time and shooting them. I was rather towards the back, having been amongst those first to enter the barn. When the men in front of myself and the others had been taken out and shot, it came on to rain, and the shooting was finished off in the barn. We were ordered to turn round, and we were then shot through the back. The man who had

begun the bombing, and had insulted Captain Lynn Allen, when he had protested, took part in this shooting. Later on, the Germans fired tommy-guns into the barn, and I was hit again and became unconscious. When I recovered, I found that my right leg had been shattered by a group of bullets from a tommy-gun, and that my left leg had also sustained a wound. I lay in the barn for from two to three days. One of the few survivors was a friend of mine, Private Jack Bennett of Abingdon Berks: who had been shot in the stomach. I could not move, but he and Private Johnson, also of The Royal Warwickshire Regiment, 'A' Company, crawled out to try and get water. A farmer came to fetch some milk cans, and was asked to give us some milk, but he refused. Subsequently, Private Bennett lay outside the barn and was noticed by two Germans with Red Cross badges, who were looking for wounded. They understood a certain amount of English, and seemed to be shocked at what had taken place. They went away and returned in about half an hour with an ambulance. By then, my friend, Private Bennett had died. The survivors of us were put into the ambulance. I do not know how far we were driven as I lost consciousness again, and I did not hear the name of the place where the dressing station was, but I recall that we were kindly treated, and that the officer in charge of the post was an elderly Surgeon with a white beard, who made a note of the statements which we made to him. After a short time, I was sent to Boulogne, and thence to Camiers where an English Surgeon, Major Martin, amputated my leg.

6.   I noticed on the uniform of the man who spoke so insultingly to Captain Lynn Allen, the badge which looks like fork lightning, and which I am informed and verily believe, is the badge worn by SS troops. I noticed this badge on the uniforms of other members of the party, including the officer who made the interrogations, and marched us to the barn.

Albert Evans

I, Albert Evans formerly, number 5184737: Private Evans of The Royal Warwickshire Regiment, now discharged from the Army, and resident at xxx , make oath and say as follows:-

1.   I belonged to 'D' Company of the 2nd Battalion:Royal Warwickshire Regiment, and was taken Prisoner on or about the 27th May 1940, at a small town or village in Belgium.

2.   At the time I was taken prisoner, I did not know the name of the place, but it was a small town or village with a square in which, to the best of my recollection and belief, was a statue of an Officer on a horse. The place was being held by the Battalion, and I have since been informed and verily believe, that the name of the place was Wormhout.

3.   We were attacked just outside the town by German tanks, and were driven back, towards a river which we could not cross, and where we were rounded up by the tanks, and taken prisoner by SS troops, who were following up behind the tanks. I took the troops to be SS troops, because, I believe they were in a black uniform with camouflaged caps, and had 'Skull and Crossbones' on their collars. They handled the prisoners extremely roughly.

4.   We were marched to a barn, and on the way the prisoners were halted to watch the houses burning in Wormhout. There were about 90 to 100 all told, in the barn, many men of The Royal Warwickshire Regiment. There was only one officer, Captain Lynn-Allen who was Commanding 'D' Company.

5.   I cannot recall clearly the course of events, but I know it was afternoon. I was standing next to Captain Lynn-Allen, just inside the door of the barn, when the Germans began throwing grenades in. I had my right arm shattered by one of the first explosions. Then, while I was still feeling dazed, and as another grenade came in through the door, Captain Lynn-Allen who, was at this time, un-wounded, seized me and dragged me out through the door, and round the corner, while the Germans who had thrown the grenades were taking cover against the explosions.

6.   Captain Lynn-Allen practically dragged or supported me the whole way to a clump of trees, which was about 200 yards away. When we got inside the trees, we found there was a small stagnant and deep pond in the centre. We got down into the pond with the water up to our chests. Captain Lynn-Allen was standing some little distance from the edge. I, because of my condition stood closer

to the bank, and presumably lower in the water. Suddenly, without warning, a German appeared on the bank of the pond just above us, showing that we must have been spotted before we gained the cover of the trees. The German who was armed with a revolver, immediately shot Captain Lynn-Allen twice. Captain Lynn-Allen's body fell forward and disappeared under the surface. The German then fired at me at a range of about three yards. I was hit twice in the neck, and already bleeding profusely from my arm, I slumped in the water. The German no doubt thought that he finished me off.

7.   I lost count of the time, but I think only for a few seconds. I was very weak, suffering considerable pain, and from shock. When I came to, the German had gone. I did not see any movement from under the water. I tried to reach under the water towards the place where Captain Allen had disappeared, but I did not find any trace of him. I waited there about twenty minutes, and then, crawling out of the pond, set off to get away.

8.   As I was clearing the trees, I was hit again in the Right shoulder not badly, with a stray bullet from the direction of the barn, where I heard considerable automatic fire going on. I crawled away down a ditch, taking what cover I could. I did not know where I was going, or how long it took, but just as it was getting dark, with my remaining strength, I crawled into another house or farm. I found that it was occupied by a German Ambulance Unit. Here, I was seen by a German Doctor, and he, and his Unit undoubtedly by their attention, saved my life, for the second time. The Doctor listened attentively to my story, as though he meant to report it.

Robert William Gill

I, Robert William Gill, Sergeant, formerly Corporal, number 5110615 Royal Warwickshire Regiment, with permanent address at xxx, make oath and say as follows:-

1.   I was captured by members of an SS Division of the Germans on the 28th of May 1940 at Wormhout, Belgium(?)

2. After capture, I was taken with four other, all of the Royal Warwickshire Regiment, to a barn. The names of the others are: Pte. TOMBS: Pte. BOX: and Pte. DALEY.

3. There were about forty-five (45) prisoners of war in the barn, including a Captain ALLEN, 2nd Battalion Royal Warwickshire Regiment. After we arrived in the barn, we were told by a German *Gefreiter* to get to the back of the barn, and at the same time, he threatened us with a stick grenade. Captain Allen thereupon went forward, at the same time pleading with the *Gefreiter* to wait a minute, but another German riddled Captain Allen with a tommy-gun and he fell. I had a look at Captain Allen a quarter of an hour later, and he appeared to me to be dead.

4. The *Gefreiter* then threw the stick grenade he was holding at us, and 5110619 Pte: *Kelly* The Royal Warwickshire Regiment, was badly wounded, his right leg being blown away.

5. The Germans then told us to get out of the barn five at a time, and as soon as the first five were outside, I saw through a hole in the back of the barn, that they were lined up about seven yards from the barn, and there were five Germans, who shot them in the back. Private Box was one of the 5 shot, but Pte: Box was the only survivor.

6. A further five were taken out of the barn, and one of those was Pte: Garside. We heard shots, and we did not see those five again.

7. When the next five were ordered out, we all refused to go, and five Germans who were in front of us in the barn, then started shooting at us with their rifles, and as a result, about twenty to twenty-five of us were killed, including Acting/C.S.M. Moore 3rd Mortar Platoon, Royal Warwickshire Regiment.

8. The Germans eventually left us, thinking we were all dead, and after they had gone, I found that besides myself, there were alive six others including Pte: Box who was outside the barn. Pte. Tombs: Pte: Townsend: Pte: Daly: and Pte: Kelly., all of the Royal Warwickshire Regiment. Pte: Townsend, Pte: Kelly, and Pte: Daly were wounded.

9. The *Gefreiter* was about 26 years of age, 5 feet 7 inches in height very dark, bronze, and I noticed the SS markings on the collar of his tunic, namely a zig-zag mark in silver, on a Green background. All

the Germans had the same markings and wore too, black and green capes. They all appeared to be drugged or intoxicated. I do not remember seeing any number on the tunics of the Germans.

10. I went with one other to endeavour to get help, to get the two wounded Pte: Kelly and Pte: Townsend away, and just after we had started, three others caught us up, namely, Pte: Tombs: Pte: Box and another Pte: Daley. There were two Privates Daly/Daley in the barn incident.

11. Whilst we were looking for help, we were ambushed, and a Private who started off with me was killed, and the rest of us were captured.

12. We were taken to a farm which appeared to be German Headquarters and I was interrogated by an *Oberleutnant* who spoke perfect English. He told me that he had been in London. He endeavoured to get military information from me, which I refused. He did not appear to know anything about the barn incident, until I told him, and he told me to keep quiet in case any of the other Germans understood English. He prevented a *Feldwebel* from striking me when I asked for a drink of water. The Farm was about 100 to 150 yards distant to the barn where the shooting took place.

13. This *Oberleutnant* was about 25 years of age, very dark, with a broad face, about 5 foot 7 inches in height, and stockily built, and was wearing a greyish cap.

John Edward Lavelle

I, John Edward Lavelle, formerly in the ranks of The Royal Warwickshire Regiment, recently discharged from the Army on Medical grounds and now residing at xxx, Make oath and say as follows:-

1. In the new year 1940, I was sent to France on draft from the Base to join the 2nd Battalion of the Royal Warwickshire Regiment. I was posted to 7 platoon: 'A' Company.

2. We were in position near Wormhout in May 1940, and on May 27th, we had Orders to withdraw. Shortly afterwards, I was captured by the Germans in front of the village.

3. A number of Prisoners of War, of all Regiments, were being collected by the Germans, who, as I was informed, and verily believe, were SS troops. We were all marched across some fields. It was raining at the time, and we thought they were putting us into a barn, to get us out of the rain, as there was some walking wounded. The barn stood by itself, about two fields away from the farm. There was an Officer in our party, he was a Captain, and had light hair. There were nearly a hundred men in the barn.

4. The Germans took two lots of five men from nearest the door, and shot them outside in the open. We could see this through cracks in the barn, which was largely of wood, I saw both groups shot.

5. There was one man left alive out of the first group. I believe this was Pte: Johnson of The Royal Warwickshire Regiment, who apparently feigned death, for I understood he was also picked up by the German Red Cross personnel. The second five were all shot and killed.

6. The third party refused to go out, and so the Germans began throwing grenades into the barn. They threw four or five grenades into the barn and these caused a lot of casualties. When this ended, everyone was lying on the ground, including myself. Then the Germans came in, and fired rifles and revolvers. I was wounded in the right ankle. I thought I had been wounded by a bullet, but when the X-ray was taken, it was found to be by a grenade.

7. The Germans then went away. All this happened on the afternoon of May 27th. There were about seven of us left alive. We remained for two or three days, I can't say exactly. We were eventually found by German troops, who took us to their dressing station. They asked us what had happened, and when we told them, one of them said, 'The swines.'

Richard Parry

I, Richard Tudor Parry, formerly Gunner, Royal Artillery, recently discharged from the Army, and now resident at xxx, make oath and say as follows:-

1.   I was among the soldiers who were captured and shot, in a barn near Wormhout on or about the 27th of May 1940.

2.   The Convoy in which my Battery, 242 battery, 69th Medium Regiment, was making for Dunkirk, was ambushed and destroyed at Wormhout. The men scattered according to orders, and I made my escape down a stream, chiefly by swimming under cover of the banks, until I arrived at the back of some large houses a little way out of Wormhout. I went into one of them in search of a map, but being unsuccessful, I left the house by the front entrance. I there ran into SS troops, and became a prisoner of war.

3.   My steel helmet, pay book and personal belongings were taken from me, and I was ordered to join a group of about Thirty (30) soldiers, who were standing against a wall, with their hands above their heads, while the SS guards, who were covering them with tommy-guns, took turns to take refreshments from a vacated cafe.

4.   I am sure they were SS-troops, because I saw for the first time the Lightning and Skull and Crossbones, which distinguish SS-troops. They also wore Black Uniforms, except for camouflaged capes.

5.   Later, we were marched for about a mile towards Wormhout, but bearing left of the town, until we reached a large field, where I estimate some Fifty (50) (British) soldiers were collected, mostly members of The Royal Warwickshire Regiment, and Cheshires, with a few members of The Royal Artillery.

6.   Later, a German Officer who looked like a Prussian, and wore a monocle, interviewed a man named (Daly/Daley) of whom I know nothing more, than that, to the best of my knowledge and belief, he is still alive. After that, we were marched for about two miles across the fields, until we arrived at a Cow Barn, into which, we were marched. As I passed through the door, I noticed two small milk churns, which were standing outside the door.

7.   No sooner were we all inside, than hand-grenades were thrown in, I counted five (5) in all. I was blown through a gap in the side of the barn by the first hand-grenade, and only my feet remained inside. I was wounded in my leg, and was unable to move. Then I heard the Germans shouting 'Raus, Raus' and I heard our boys shouting abuse, and later, asking if they could have a smoke, before

they were shot. Their request was apparently not granted, because a few seconds later, five men were lined up in the field on my side of the barn, and shot in the back. Then five were lined up in the field on the far side of the barn. I could see them round the back of the barn, and their last act, was to turn of their own accord, and face the firing squad.

8.   After this, the Germans stood at the barn entrance, and sprayed the wounded with tommy-guns. I was shot through the foot. This rendered me unconscious for a time, and when I awoke, I saw a German looking at me from near the barn. He lifted his tommy-gun to his shoulder, and as I tried to get to my feet, shot me through the face.

9.   When I came too, it was evening, and all was still. Two Frenchmen came to the barn, presumably to collect the milk churns, but when they saw the mess inside, they ran away. Two days later, I was picked up with others, by a Unit of the German Medical Corps, who treated us well. They put us six or seven survivors on stretchers, and took us via the clearing station, to Boulogne. I heard later, that they dug a mass grave for the dead, close to the Barn.

10.   If I was taken to Wormhout, I think I could find the barn. I also think that I could recognise the German Officer, and I am certain that I could recognise the soldier who shot me through the face. I saw a British Captain among our party, but I knew nothing about him.

Equivalent Ranks

SS	British Army
Reichsführer-SS	Field Marshal
SS-Oberstgruppenführer	General
SS-Obergruppenführer	Lieutenant-General
SS-Gruppenführer	Major-General
SS-Brigadeführer	Brigadier
SS-Oberführer	Senior Colonel
SS-Standartenführer	Colonel
SS-Obersturmbannführer	Lieutenant-Colonel
SS-Sturmbannführer	Major
SS-Hauptsturmführer	Captain
SS-Obersturmführer	Lieutenant
SS-Untersturmführer	2nd Lieutenant
SS-Sturmscharführer	Regimental Sergeant-Major
SS-Hauptscharführer	Sergeant-Major
SS-Oberscharführer	Quartermaster-Sergeant
SS-Scharführer	Staff Sergeant
SS-Unterscharführer	Sergeant
SS-Rottenführer	Corporal
SS-Sturmmann	Lance-Corporal
SS-Oberschütze	Senior Private
SS-Schütze	Private

The 2nd Battalion, Royal Warwickshire Regiment
Regimental Appointments at the Battle of Hollain,
River Escaut May 20th & 21st 1940

HQ: CO   Lt. Col. P. D. W. Dunn, DSO, MC
(evacuated, sick)

2nd. i/c	Major P. H. W. Hicks, MC
Adjutant	Capt. L. T. Tomes
I.O.	2nd. Lieut. J. Vaudrey
Q.M.	Lt. J. Williams
O.C. HQ Coy.	Major Rance, MC
Signals Officer	Lt. D. G. Padfield
MTO	2nd. Lieut. Davies
Carriers	2nd. Lieut. D. Lee (wounded)
A.A	PSM Dixon
Mortars	Sgt. Cruickshank (killed)
Pioneers	PSM Jeal
CSM HQ	PSM Chambers
RSM	RSM Turner
RQMS	RQMS Thomas
MO	Capt. A. Crook, RAMC
Liaison Officer, Brigade.	2nd. Lieut. H. Smythe
O. i/c A/Tk. Pltn.	2nd. Lieut. Schooling (wounded)

'A' Company   Major H. Harborne
Major C. Chichester-Constable, MC
2nd. Lieut. P. Chapman
2nd. Lieut. Wright
CSM Jones
PSM Bennett

'B' Company   Capt. E. Jerram
                2nd. Lieut. B. L. Gunnell
                CSM French
                Lt. Dunwell
                2nd. Lieut. P. Waterworth   (wounded)
                PSM Agutter

'C' Company   Capt. C. H. Nicholson
                Capt. J. F. Lynn-Allen
                CSM Bates
                2nd. Lieut. Gammidge   (killed)
                2nd. Lieut. Dirks
                PSM Rotton

'D' Company   Major P. Morley   (killed)
                Capt. M. E. Fisher   (wounded)
                CSM Jennings
                2nd. Lieut. Goodliffe   (wounded & POW)
                PSM Perkins   (killed)

2nd Battalion Royal Warwickshire Regiment
Regimental Appointments, Wormhout, 28th May 1940

HQ: CO   Major P. H. W. Hicks, MC
                Major H. Harborne
                   (wounded & POW)
    Adjutant   Captain L. T. Tomes
                   (wounded & POW)
    IO   2nd. Lieut. J. L. Vaudrey
    QM   Lieut. S. J. Williams
    OC HQ Company   Major Rance, MC   (killed)
    Signals Officer   Sergeant Bell
MTO 2nd. Lieut. Davies
      O i/c Carriers   Sgt. Roddis
      Mortars   None left in action
      A.A   PSM Dixon

Pioneers   PSM Jeal (POW)
R.S.M   RSM Turner
RQMS   RQMS Thomas
CSM   PSM Chambers
MO   Captain A. Crook, RAMC
       (POW)

LO Brigade   2nd Lieut. M Smythe
Agent de Liaison Sergeant Georges Coulon

'A' Company Major C. Chichester-Constable MC (killed)
      Captain D. G. Padfield (killed)
      CSM Jones (wounded & POW)
      2nd Lieut. P. Chapman (wounded)
      2nd Lieut. Wright
      PSM Bennett

'B' Company Captain E. J. Jerram
      2nd Lieut. B. L. Gunnell (POW)
      CSM French (POW)
      Lieut. Dunwell (killed)
      PSM Agutter (killed)

'C' Company Captain C. H. Nicholson
      CSM Bates
      2nd Lieut. Dirks (wounded)
      PSM Rotton

('C' Company was withdrawn on May 27th to guard Div. HQ at Bergues)

'D' Company Captain J. F. Lynn-Allen (killed)
      2nd Lieut. J. W. Tomes
      CSM Jennings (killed)
      PSM Gladwyn
      PSM Hughes (killed)

SS Leibstandarte Adolf Hitler Regiment
Regimer :al Appointments during the Battle of Wormhout [1]

Regimental-		
Commander		Josef 'Sepp' Dietrich
Adjutant		Wilhelm Keilhau
2nd Adjutant		Wünsche
Asst. Adjutant		Günter Scheiner
Asst. Adjutant		Eric Maas
I.D. Officer		Walter Ewart

1st Battalion

OC		Kohlroser
Adjutant		Malinowsky (killed)
Commander	1st Coy.	Horst Meier
	2nd Coy.	Hans Meisorch (killed)
	3rd Coy.	Heinrich Schuldt (killed)
	4th Coy.	Riester (killed)

2nd Battalion

OC		Schützeck (wounded)
Adjutant		Bütler
Commander	5th Coy.	Wilhelm Mohnke (Acting C.O.)
	6th Coy.	Anhlat
	7th Coy.	Baum
	8th Coy.	Horstmann (killed)

[1] As supplied by Eric Maas, from memory.

3rd Battalion

OC		Trabandt (Senior Battalion Commander)
Adjutant		Stein
Commander	9th Coy.	Mauersberg
	10th Coy.	Weidenhaupt
	11th Coy.	Marcks
	12th Coy.	Garthe
	13th Coy.	Schroeder (killed)
	14th Coy.	Hanreich
	15th Coy.	Kurt Meyer ('Panzermeyer')
	16th Coy.	Szdzetosek

At Wormhout, the Regiment was supported by a Panzer Unit of the German Army.

The Intelligence Summary for the 2nd Battalion Royal
Warwickshire Regiment, reads as follows:–
From 0700 hours 28th May to 29th May 1940

1 *Enemy Order of Battle*

Enemy attacked with large numbers of tanks from every direction. Tanks were large and were closely followed and, in many
cases, actually accompanied by infantry. Tanks advanced at a slow
pace firing continually with machine-guns using tracer bullets, and
also from a larger gun firing small shells.

Infantry

Attacked in large numbers and, in some cases, shoulder to
shoulder. In rear they were urged on by the cry of 'Heil, Hitler!'
Large numbers were undoubtedly mown down by our fire. At one
point, a charge was made with fixed bayonets.

Dress

Many of the enemy were dressed in civilian clothes, others wore
uniforms of the British, French and Belgian Armies. As they came
they shouted: 'Hullo, boys! We're here, don't fire'.

2 *Enemy Artillery Activity*

0700 – 1200   Intermittently fired on by enemy mortars.

1200 –   Shelled by heavy guns with accuracy. Four or five
large salvos landed right on HQ Company where 'A' Echelon
Transport was parked.

3 *Enemy Air Activity*

0900   Visit by usual recce plane.

0910   15 bombers appeared and heavily bombed 'A' Company's
position.

Further activity negligible.

SOURCES

Notes on Sources

Chapter 1
The Order of the Death's Head, Heinz Hohne (Secker & Warburg)
p. 404
The Waffen SS, George Stein (Cornell University Press)   p. 4
Hitler, A Study in Tyranny, A. Bullock (Odhams)   p. 228 .
Die Waffen SS, Walter Gorlitz (Arani Verlag)   p. 9
Die Armee der Geachteten, Felix Steiner (Plesse
Verlag, Gottingen)   p. 70
Material on Dietrich, extra to above:
The Weiner Library, London

Chapter 2
The Regimental History of the Royal Warwickshire Regiment pp. 15-26
The War Diaries of the 2nd Battalion, Royal Warwicks
Records Office, London
The Second World War, Winston Churchill (Cassell) paper-back ed.
vol 3 ch. 1
The Collapse of the Third Republic, William Shirer (Heinemann)
chs. 28, 29
The History of the Second World War, Liddell Hart (Cassell) ch. 4
Destination Dunkirk, Gregory Blaxland (William Kimber)   ch. 6

Eye-witness accounts:
Arthur Johnson
George Hall

'Personal Diary' Capt. L. T. Tomes (Privately Published)

Chapter 3
The Regimental History
The War Diaries

Personal History of Tomes

Eye-witness account:—
W. Cordrey

Chapter 4
The History of the Second World War, B. Liddell Hart   chs. 2 & 7
The Collapse of the Third Republic, W. Shirer   ch. 30
A Concise History of Warfare, Field Marshal Montgomery (Collins)
ch. 19
The Rise & Fall of the Third Reich, W. Shirer (Secker & Warburg)
chs. 19 & 20
The Waffen SS, G. Stein   p. 150
Death of an Army, A. Farrar-Hockley (Arthur Barker) (Schlieffen
Plan)   ch. 1
The Origins of the Second World War, A. J. P. Taylor (Hamish
Hamilton)   chs. 1 & 11
France and Belgium 1939-1940, Brian Bond, (Davis Poynter)
chs. 1 & 2

Chapter 5
Regimental History   Relevant period
Battalion Diary   Relevant period
Battalion Diary, 5th Gloucestershire Regiment,
   (Public Records Office)   Relevant Period
Personal Diary of Tomes   Relevant period
War Diary of 4th Cheshire Regiment
   (Public Records Office)   Relevant period
War Diary of 8th Worcestershire Regiment
   (Public Records Office)   Relevant period
                                               Relevant period

Personal Account:
A. Evans

Chapter 6
The Rise and Fall of the Third Reich, W. Shirer   ch. 21
Panzer Leader, Guderian (Michael Joseph)   p. 151

The History of the Second World War, B. Liddell Hart   ch. 7
Personal accounts by:
SS-Oberführer Otto Baum
SS-Oberstgruppenführer Dietrich
SS-Sturmbannführer Eric Maas
SS-Obersturmbannführer Bütler
Regimental History, Warwicks.
Battalion Diary, Warwicks.
'B' Company Diary, 2nd Battalion Warwicks
Personal Diary, Tomes
Battalion Intelligence Report

Chapter 7
Personal accounts by:
A. Evans
Oskar Schauff
R. Parry
G. Hall
A. Tombs
C. Daley
R. West

Personal Diary, Tomes
Battalion War Diary
Regimental History

Personal account by:
W. Cordrey

Chapter 8
Personal accounts by:
R. West
G. Merry
A. Evans
R. Parry
J. Lavelle

A. Tombs
G. Hopper
G. Hall
A. Ebner

Chapter 9
Personal accounts by:
G. Hopper
A. Tombs
R. West
G. Hall
A. Montague
Koriaka
F. Bütler
O. Baum
A. Johnson
L. Carrier
War Diary 5th Gloucesters
Intelligence Summary 2nd Battalion Royal Warwicks

Chapter 10
Personal account by:
C. Daley
Information from:
R. Parry
Local sources at Esquelbecq
War Graves Commission
The Vengeance of Private Pooley, Victor Gollancz
Information supplied to author by Mr W. O'Callaghan and
Mme Creton

Chapter 11
Information supplied by:
G. Hall
R. West

Chapter 12
Waffen SS, John Keegan (Pan/Ballantine)   pp. 67-69
The Order of the Death's Head, Heinz Hohne   p. 427
The History of the Second World War, B. Liddell Hart   chs. 18, 28
A Concise History of Warfare, Field Marshal Montgomery pp. 320-322
The Last 100 Days, John Toland (Arthur Barker)   p. 338
The Rise and Fall of the Third Reich, W. Shirer   p. 1005
The Bormann Brotherhood, William Stevenson (Arthur Barker)
Massacre at Malmedy, Charles Whiting (Leo Cooper)
Caen: Anvil of Victory, Alexander McKee (Souvenir Press, London)

Chapter 13
Information by:
Mrs. M. Tombs
Mrs. K. West
R. Parry
C. Daley
Sunday Pictorial (21.11.1943)
A. Evans
The Vengeance of Private Pooley
Letters to Parry

Chapter 14
The Trial of Kurt Meyer, J. A. MacDonald (Irwin, Toronto)
The London Cage, A. Scotland (Evans Bros.)
Information by:
Ebner
Schauff
Koriaka
Smidt
Baum
Hasenwinkel
Kummert
A. Tombs
A. Evans

Massacre at Malmedy, Charles Whiting   p 215 & chs. 11, 12, 13
The Rise and Fall of the Third Reich, Shirer   p. 1095

Bibliography

Books

Blaxland, G., *Destination Dunkirk*, William Kimber
Bond, B., *France and Belgium 1939-40*, Davis-Poynter
Bullock, A., *Hitler, A Study in Tyranny*, Odhams
Churchill, W., *The Second World War*, Cassell
Farrar-Hockley, A. H., *Death of An Army*, Arthur Barker
Gorlitz, W., *Die Waffen SS*, Arani Verlag
Guderian, *Panzer Leader*, Michael Joseph
Hart Liddell, B., *The History of the Second World War*, Cassell
Höhne, H., *The Order of the Death's Head*, Secker & Warburg
Jolley, C., *The Vengeance of Private Pooley*, Gollancz
Keegan, J., *Waffen-SS*, Pan/Ballantine
MacDonald, J. A., *The Trial of Kurt Meyer*, Irwin, Toronto
McKee, A., *Caen: Anvil of Victory*, Souvenir Press
Montgomery, B., *A Concise History of Warfare*, Collins
Scotland, A., *The London Cage*, Evans
Shirer, W., *The Collapse of the Third Republic*, Heineman
Shirer, W., *The Rise and Fall of the Third Reich*, Secker & Warburg
Stein, G., *The Waffen SS*, Cornell University Press
Steiner, F., *Die Armee der Geachteten*, Plesse Verlag Gottingen
Stevenson, W., *The Bormann Brotherhood*, Arthur Barker/Corgi
Taylor, J., *The Origins of the Second World War*, Hamish Hamilton
Toland, J., *The Last Hundred Days*, Arthur Barker
Trevor-Roper, H., *The Last Days of Hitler*, Macmillan
Wenn Alle Brüder Schweigen (German publication)
Whiting, C., *Massacre at Malmedy*, Cooper

Other Sources

War Diaries: 2nd Battalion, Royal Warwickshire Regiment
               2nd Battalion, 'B' Company
               Intelligence Summary, May 28th 1940
               5th Gloucestershire Regiment
               4th Cheshire Regiment
               8th Worcestershire Regiment
Regimental History, Royal Warwickshire Regiment
Private Diary of Captain L. T. Tomes (Privately Published)

Crimes Alleged to have been Committed
by Waffen-SS Units

SS-LEIBSTANDARTE ADOLF HITLER (LSSAH)

Unit	Date and place	Incident	Source
Musikzug	25.9.39 *Burzeum*	Murder of 50 Jews	AG 3/VY PWIS/LDC/510
2nd Battn	Sept 39 *Lodz*	Pillage, torture of civilians	UNWCC 284/P/G/29
	Sept 39 *Zdunska Wola*	Torture of civilians	UNWCC 284/P/G/29
	Oct 39 *Grojec*	Pillage, confiscation of property	UNWCC 284/P/G/29
	Oct 39 *Czestochowa*	Massacre	UNWCC 284/P/G/29
	28.5.40 *Wormhout*	British POWs shot	
	1941 *Zhitomir*	Mass murder of Jews	PWIS(H)/ LDC/510,299
2nd Regt	Spring 1943 *Nr Kharkov*	Staroverovka burnt	AG 3/VW PWIS(H)/LDC/395
	Spring 1943 *Nr Kharkov*	Stanitschnoje burnt	AG 3/VW PWIS(H)/LDC/395
Recce Battn	Spring 1943 *Nr Kharkov*	Jefremovka burnt, civilian population murdered	AG 3/VW PWIS(H)/LDC/395
	March 1943 *Nr Kharkov*	Smyev burnt, all inhabitants murdered	AG 3/VW
2nd Regt 3 Battn	Oct 1943 *Nr Toreno*	Village burnt	AG 3/VW

Whole Division	1943 *Russia*	Order given to Division that in case of capture all villages be evacuated & burnt	PWIS(H)/ LDC/510
6th Pz Gren Regt 2	20.8.44 *Nr Paris*	Houses burnt, French civilians murdered at St D	PWIS(H)/ LDC/622
	25.8.44	Australian flyer and others murdered	SHAEF
	6.9.44 *Navaugle, Nr Marche*	Entire village burnt Woman shot attempting to escape Shooting of hostages	
	5.9.44	Pillage, wanton destruction of property	1573/B/G/127 (UNWCC)
	7.9.44 *Nerstal, Nr Liege*	Hostages shot Forced labour	1810/B/G/163 (UNWCC)
	24.8.44 *Leshogues*	5 Allied POWs shot	AG 3/VW
1st Pz Regt	20.12.44 *Stavelot, Belgium*	Mass murder	898/B/G/61 (UNWCC)

Decorations

Awards were made to the following officers and other ranks for their participation in the Battle of Wormhout:

Lt Colonel P. H. W. Hicks, MC   DSO
Major E. J. Jerram   MC
Captain C. H. Nicholson   MC
2nd Lieut H. Smythe   MC
2nd Lieut B. L. Gunnell   MC
(This officer was recommended for the VC but three witnesses were not available)
CQ MS Wyeth   DCM
Sgt Bell   MM
(acting Signals Officer after murder of Captain Padfield)

(Information supplied 28.7.1977 by Colonel E. J. Jerram, MC).

Index

217